Here's A Wonderful Opportunity To Help Your Child Grow As A Reader

"...chock full of information f⌐   ing skills and attaining reading enjov⌐   'AL

"...a terrific book!...sʰ   ᴜ make reading fun."
       ᴜ ɪ IC MAGAZINES

"...a tremendous resource book for parents...shows numerous ways to help a child develop reading skills at home."
MELANIE D. HALL, *Coordinator*
Philadelphia Parents Union

"...shows how to make reading fun-damental."
FAMILY WEEKLY

"...your child's first giant step towards being a better reader "
YOUNG PARENTS BOOK CLUB

"...shows how to help children discover the joy of reading."
NEW YORK DAILY NEWS

"...answers actual questions parents have about children's reading."
DR. DOROTHY RICH, *President*
The Home and School Institute

"...tells how to produce super readers...shows how parents can make learning a pleasure."
ALBERT SHANKER, *President*
American Federation of Teachers

Your child can be a

At last! A fun and easy approach to reading improvement.

by Len Kusnetz

illustrations by
Shelley Kusnetz

LEARNING HOUSE PUBLISHERS
Roslyn Heights ● New York

Published by LEARNING HOUSE PUBLISHERS
38 South Street, Roslyn Heights, NY 11577

*(Learning House Books are available at special discounts
to schools and parent groups. For information write
Special Sales, Learning House Publishers, 38 South St.,
Roslyn Heights, NY 11577)*

Distributed to the trade by Liberty Publishing Company,
50 Scott Adam Road, Cockeysville, MD 21030

Cover Design by Tom Yohe
Book Design by North Shore Graphic Arts

PRINTED IN THE UNITED STATES OF AMERICA

Library of Congress Cataloging in Publication Data

Kusnetz, Len.
    Your child can be a super reader: a fun and easy
approach to reading improvement.

    Includes bibliographical references and index.
    1. Books and reading for children. 2. Children's
literature — Bibliography. I. Kusnetz, Shelley.
II. Title.
Z1037.A1K87   028.5'5
ISBN 0-9602730-0-X
Library of Congress Catalog Number 79-84790

For Roni, Philip, and Jody
. . . and children everywhere

Acknowledgements

"Camaro Interiors" appears through the courtesy of the Chevrolet Motor Division, General Motors Corporation.

"Michael & Maple & Brown Sugar" appears through the courtesy of the Quaker Oats Company.

The excerpt from "Scandal Sheet" from an *Archie at Riverdale High* Magazine is reproduced here with the permission of Archie Enterprises, Inc.

The excerpt from "The Trenchcoat Brigade" is reprinted here through the courtesy of United Press International.

The recipe "from Sweden Meat Balls" is from *MANY HANDS COOKING: An International Cookbook for Girls and Boys* by Terry Touff Cooper and Marilyn Ratner. Text Copyright© 1974 by Terry Touff Cooper and Marilyn Ratner. By permission of Thomas Y. Crowell.

The author also thanks Judy C. Shevrin, a reading specialist in the New York City Public School System, for her valuable help in the preparation of this book.

You may notice that your child is referred to as "he" in this book. This has been done solely to make the book more readable, as the phrase "he or she" would be tedious to read over and over again. It is hoped that no parent feels slighted by the word "he" as it is clearly meant to include boys and girls.

Contents

Special Note To Parents

Dear Parent,

Reading is a wonderful activity for children. Books open the door to adventure, and bring young readers a world of fun and excitement. Discovering new ideas and new experiences in books also helps young people understand more about themselves and their own lives.

Unfortunately, many of our children do not enjoy reading. These youngsters feel that reading is a chore in school, and an activity to be avoided at home. Children who don't develop positive feelings about reading are likely to make slow progress and be underachievers all through school.

The idea behind this book is that parents can help their children discover the joy of reading. You will find many outstanding books and magazines described here that match your child's special interests and needs. You can use these lists to select just the right reading materials to spark your child's imagination and make reading fun.

The book also features an enjoyable reading program designed to give children in grades 3 through 9 a new chance to develop their reading skills to the highest level. Complete, step-by-step instructions show how to help your child read more quickly, easily, and with better understanding. Using this method, you can give your child new power and confidence in reading right in your own home.

This book invites you to join in your school's efforts to help your child grow as a reader. All of the information contained here is easy-to-follow and requires no special background in reading on your part. If you are willing to give your child ten to fifteen minutes of your time each day, you can make a tremendous contribution to the most important part of his education. Here is a wonderful opportunity to make reading fun and rewarding for your child!

With best wishes,

Len Kusnetz

1
How This
Book Will
Help You

Boys and girls who don't like to read have a difficult time in school. They often get low marks because they have trouble understanding their work. Textbooks, class notes, homework assignments, and test questions confuse these children. They are identified as "average" or "below average" students, and these labels damage their self-respect.

Schools try to help these children improve their reading skills in special reading classes or reading labs. Some parents decide to get professional help for their children outside of school. These parents spend hundreds of dollars for reading tutors to come to their homes, or for private lessons for their children at local reading development centers or clinics.

Unfortunately, these solutions do not usually turn underachieving or reluctant readers into good readers. Remedial reading programs emphasize "catching up" in ability, rather than "pulling ahead." Children sometimes feel they are forced to participate in these programs. They work and learn to be set free from their embarrassment and the monotony of reading drills.

Remedial reading programs often fail to change children's attitudes toward reading. When the programs end, the children still feel that reading is an unpleasant activity they are forced to do, not something they want to do.

Teachers know that the best readers have just the opposite attitude about reading. They love to read outside of school for their own personal enjoyment. No teacher ever has to force these children to read!

Why do the children who read a lot wind up with the best reading skills? Here is their secret. As they read, they come across and learn new vocabulary words. It is this **WORD POWER** which makes them the best readers, and gives them advantages over other students. When a teacher, textbook, or test uses "new words," these children already know them.

Going to reading lab is no fun.

Should a parent put pressure on a child to read a lot of books? No! A child must feel that reading is exciting and enjoyable. Only then will he read because he wants to read. When a child enjoys reading for pleasure, he will be on the way to becoming a superior reader.

This guide will show you how to help your child become an eager and accomplished reader. You will learn how your child can read a variety of irresistible books and build powerful vocabulary and reading skills the way the best readers do. Most important of all, those books will make reading fun.

This book does not show you how to teach your child to sound out or pronounce words. (This method is called "phonics"). It is assumed that your child is learning, or will learn these skills in school.

Your Child Can Be a Super Reader will show you how to help your child develop a positive, enthusiastic attitude toward books and learning. This guide also includes information on how to begin a reading improvement program for children in grades 3–9. By providing a series of delightful reading experiences at home, you can increase reading enjoyment and raise your child's reading ability to its highest potential.

The program has been designed so that your child will do most of the work himself. Your role is to give encouragement and support, and just a few minutes of your time each day.

WORD POWER is the key to reading success.

Your time and effort will be one of the greatest gifts you could ever give your youngster. New word power and good reading habits will help your child to:

- do well in school
- score high on reading tests
- read, enjoy, and understand more
- gain self-confidence

Your child will appreciate your help. He knows that reading is the basic tool of learning in school. Helping your child grow as a reader is a great way to help him get the most out of his education!

2

Raising Readers
At Home

Learning to read is one of the most important steps your child will ever take. As a concerned parent, you want to be sure that your child's first experiences with words and books are happy and successful. Learning that books are friends and that words have magic will carry into the school years and make a world of difference in the years to come.

You can give your child a wonderful start in reading at home.

The preschool years provide a great opportunity to give your child a wonderful first-start in reading. Young children are curious about their world and have adventurous minds and imaginations just waiting for new experiences. It's really a natural time to share adventures with storybook characters and learn about people, places, animals, and things. When you read to a young child, he also hears new words and sees them in print. The colorful illustrations in books widen a child's world as well as bring joy and laughter.

You can really help your child develop a positive attitude at home toward reading. Children learn by imitation, and if your son or daughter sees you reading books, magazines, or newspapers, the message is clear that reading is an important part of your family life. Research done by colleges and universities shows that children who become achievers in school come from homes where parents place importance on reading for pleasure.

Television and Reading

The amount of time your family spends watching TV can have a lot to do with how successful a reader your child becomes. Television is sometimes criticized by educators for several reasons. Surveys show that the average preschooler in America watches nearly 30 hours of TV during the week! Children who watch that much television as they grow up are learning not to reach for books as a source of pleasure. In addition, when a young child sits quietly in front of a set, you can't really know if he understands what he sees and hears on the screen. Many young children barely make sense out of those rapidly-changing sights and sounds. This is not good preparation for becoming a successful reader. When children enter school, many have been so captivated by TV that they have difficulty sitting and learning for periods of time in a classroom where the teacher can't be changed by turning a channel selector!

What can parents do? Parents can set a good example for their children by being selective, choosing good shows, and watching TV in moderation. Your family certainly should watch favorite programs, but you might want to eliminate the shows that family members agree are not "really good." You might have your family get together to decide what shows will be watched during the coming week. If there is a block of time between two of your favorite shows, it's a good idea to turn off the set during that time.

Here are some additional guidelines you may find helpful when it comes to watching TV in your home:

- Don't use your TV set as a babysitter when you're not with your child. If your child is watching the set by himself, the show should be educational.
- Don't use TV as a reward for good behavior. You want to make your child less attached to your set.
- If your child wants to watch TV because he is bored, suggest other activities or projects he will enjoy.
- Encourage your child to ask questions about new words or ideas that are not clear in his mind. In this way you can make watching TV a learning experience.
- Turn off "junk" and encourage your child to do the same. Your family time is limited, so don't waste it on bad TV shows.

Have your family decide what shows to watch during the coming week.

- If older children watch a show that deals with a controversial topic, use that as a starting point for a family discussion.
- Nights without TV should be accepted as normal and routine in your home.

Family Reading Time

With TV-watching under control in your home, you will have time left over for other worthwhile family activities. A daily family reading time can be as cozy and satisfying as watching TV, and will also improve the quality of your family's life together. Your child will look forward with pleasure to a special time when family members come together to hear an exciting story read aloud or have a quiet individual reading time. After either kind of reading activity, your family can talk about and share highlights from what has been read.

Reading bedtime stories is a very special time of sharing between a parent and child. Enjoying a book together is a wonderful way to finish your child's day. Children love when parents read to them, and you can start as soon as your child is old enough to hold a picture book in his hands. As your child learns to read, encourage him to read to you. Most boys and girls are thrilled to show off their newly-acquired skills to their parents, the most important people in the world to them.

This special reading time does not have to always be at bedtime. You could read after breakfast, before going shopping or naptime, as a quiet time after school, or while dinner is cooking. Whenever you read aloud, sit close together so you both can see the pictures and words on the page. Be ready to read your child's favorite books over and over again for certain storybook characters are bound to become your child's close friends.

If you are reading a new book to your child, allow some extra time for questions and discussion. Take a relaxed approach and try to relate your child's own experiences to the characters, events, and pictures in the story. You should also be sure not to force a book on your child if he doesn't like it, for reading books together should be wonderful fun.

*Reading stories at bedtime will delight
your child.*

Choosing Books for Children

Bookstores and libraries contain an amazing array of books
which, at first, look very similar to an adult. In choosing first
books for your child, keep in mind his age and his special interests. Try to select books that have funny, entertaining stories,
with plenty of action and lifelike characters, clear pictures, and
short, easy-to-follow sentences. If your child enjoys a particular
author, series, or type of book, try to bring home similar books
in the future. Avoid books with too many hard words for your
child to understand.

For your convenience, a recommended list of very popular books for both preschoolers and older children has been included in Chapter 8 of this book. You can find additional worthwhile books for your child by asking librarians, booksellers, or teachers to make further suggestions. Many excellent and inexpensive children's books can also be bought in toy stores, supermarkets, and variety stores or through mail-order children's book clubs.

Your child will be proud of his books and will enjoy keeping them together on a shelf or in a small bookcase in his room. As your child becomes older, he will enjoy choosing a book from his own personal library to read with you or by himself. At some point, your child will want to select books to add to his collection. When your child is strongly attracted to a particular book, buy it for him if possible.

The first books that you read with your child will help prepare him to learn to read well. Right from the start, your son or daughter will enjoy the vivid illustrations, and learn to recognize some basic words. As those words become familiar, your child will learn to associate them with the action in the pictures. In time, your preschooler may memorize an entire story and be able to "read" or recite that book for you! Your child will hopefully then begin to recognize those same words on pages of other books, and have a real head-start in reading.

Sharing Words With Children

Many reading experts believe that there is another important factor that helps promote "reading readiness" in young children. The idea is that the more experiences a boy or girl has hearing or using language, the easier it will be to learn to read. Reading aloud is only one way to share language with your child. Preparing your child to be a good reader actually takes place every time you talk to a young child and pay attention to what he has to say about things.

Children who are good talkers learn to read and write more easily. The early years provide a great opportunity to help your child feel at ease with using language through family conversations. You might want to take advantage of some of the following activities to increase your child's word and language experiences as he grows:

- Recite nursery rhymes or sing songs like "Old MacDonald Had a Farm."
- Take your child places that will help give him new interests. You can visit museums, zoos, a children's theater, take bus and train rides, or find other exciting things to do.
- Make up stories about friendly animals to tell your child, and encourage him to help you continue the story.
- Teach your child to print the letters in his name, then encourage him to practice with the other letters in the alphabet.
- Label pictures your child draws and let him copy the words you write.
- Get ideas from educational TV shows such as *Sesame Street*. When your child says the word "Daddy," you can ask what sound the word begins with.
- Label objects in your child's room.
- Take advantage of everyday events to teach your child basic words. Words like "push" and "pull" on doors, and names of supermarkets or gas stations, are easy first words for a child to learn.
- While dinner is cooking, have your child make a menu for "Mommy's Kitchen" by spelling all the items you plan to serve.
- Let your child cut up old magazines and paste pictures of animals or objects on paper to make his own books. Help by spelling the words he wants on each page.
- If you own a casette tape recorder, record some of your child's favorite stories. When your child learns to read, let him record himself reading. You can also then record a story together, by reading alternate paragraphs or taking the parts of different characters.

Your child's language experiences will help him prepare for learning to read and write well in school. Keep in mind, however, that all children learn at different rates. Many children pick up reading later than others and then show a real burst in ability level. It's a good idea not to pressure your child to hurry and learn to read before his time. A child who is relaxed is more likely to learn to read than a child who is under stress.

As a parent, you will be your child's first teacher and a major influence upon him. You can feel confident that you can enrich your youngster's life by helping him to discover books and by developing his ability to recognize and use words. By encouraging a lifelong love of reading and learning, you will also be giving your child a firm foundation for a happy, productive future.

3

Good Reading:
The Key To
School Success!

Nothing is more important for success in school than the ability to read well. Good reading skills enable a child to make rapid progress and learn as much as he possibly can in all subjects. These vital skills can make every one of a child's days in school a rich, productive, and enjoyable experience.

Teachers are delighted to find good readers in their classes. These children are generally recognized as the best students in school. Their reading skills enable them to learn all subjects at a rapid pace. Usually, the best readers are able to earn the highest marks.

Poor readers, on the other hand, often feel uncomfortable in school. These youngsters have to struggle for good grades, as most learning is accomplished through reading. Children with weak reading skills know they have failed to meet the standards set by the school, and often form a negative attitude toward school and learning in general.

Schools are committed to helping each child develop his abilities to the fullest potential. Many schools try to meet this goal by organizing classes according to children's reading ability. Most educators believe that ability grouping places each student in the best possible classroom situation. In this way, an entire class can be taught at approximately the same pace.

Schools also provide remedial classes for students who need help in reading. While some students appreciate the opportunity to become better readers, others feel that being scheduled for remedial reading means they are "dumb". Unfortunately, schools must find time in a student's program for extra reading help by omitting other enriching subjects such as foreign language, art, music, or shop class.

Children do have the opportunity to leave average or bottom classes. The school will advance a child with good report card marks and a good reading test score into a higher class when the new Fall term begins.

UNDERSTANDING READING TEST SCORES

Teachers, guidance counselors, and school administrators are tremendously interested in their students' reading test scores. These tests are designed to measure how well a child reads compared to other children in the same grade. Many schools actually place a greater importance on a child's reading test scores than on report card marks to determine class placement.

Reading test results are easy to understand. Children's scores

Schools are tremendously interested
in students' reading test scores.

are usually given in *grade equivalents.* Suppose a child scores 6.3 ("six point three") on a reading test. These numbers mean that the child reads as well as an "average" child in the third month of the sixth grade. (The first number shows the child's grade ability, while the second number indicates the month of that school year).

Let's look at some sample scores in the same way a school would. Here are three children's test scores for the past two years:

	test scores in 6th grade	test scores in 7th grade
Michael	6.2	8.5
Jennifer	6.7	7.8
Scott	4.6	4.9

Schools expect that a student's reading ability will go up at least one year in a year's time. Of our three students, Michael has clearly made the greatest reading progress over the past year. He has improved from 6.2 (sixth grade, second month) to 8.5 (eighth grade, fifth month). These scores represent an improvement of 2.3 years ability (or two years, three months) in only one year's time (8.5 − 6.2 = 2.3).

Jennifer has improved 1.1 years over the past year (7.8 − 6.7 = 1.1).

Scott shows the least improvement. His reading score has increased only .3 years (or three months) since the last test (4.9 − 4.6 = .3).

Michael and Jennifer show satisfactory improvement in reading ability over the past year. Scott's score, however, shows that he is falling behind in reading ability.

Children who read a great deal often raise their reading levels by as much as two or three years in one year's time! Reading tests are easy for good readers. Their knowledge of words helps them to understand the questions and to get many right answers. On the other hand, children who don't read at home do poorly on reading tests.

Here are some vocabulary and reading comprehension questions from a sample reading test. These tests are divided into two parts — a vocabulary section and a reading comprehension section. A child's reading level is found by averaging his scores on these two parts of the test. You can see that a child with a powerful vocabulary has a great advantage on both parts of a reading test.

The *vocabulary section* measures a child's word knowledge. The child must select the correct meaning for each of approximately fifty words. The test is constructed so that easy words are given in the beginning. The words become increasingly more difficult as the test goes on.

Here are ten sample vocabulary questions designed for junior high school students:

1. a **daisy** is . . . a) an insect   b) a flower   c) a bird   d) a bush

2. to **hammer** is to . . . a) drill   b) cut   c) smooth   d) hit

3. a **scent** is a . . . a) coin   b) package   c) smell   d) sound

4. **loyal** means . . . a) faithful   b) unfair   c) lovable   d) usual

5. to **descend** is to . . . a) jump   b) trip   c) travel   d) fall

6. **grimy** means . . . a) dirty   b) wrinkled   c) ripped   d) rough

7. **fragile** means . . . a) bendable   b) breakable   c) blendable
d) believable

8. an **anthem** is a . . . a) pledge   b) prayer   c) song   d) theme

9. **celestial** means . . . a) musical   b) heavenly   c) restful
d) benign

10. **palatial** means . . . a) palatable   b) extravagant   c) romantic
d) ostentatious

Answers: 1. b   2. d   3. c   4. a   5. d   6. a   7. b   8. c   9. b
10. b

The best readers score high on this section because they are familiar with the vocabulary words appearing on the test.

The *reading comprehension section* measures how well a child understands what he reads. The child must answer a series of questions about six or seven different reading selections. *It is not possible for a child with a weak vocabulary to get a high score on the reading comprehension part of the test. A child must know what words mean before he can understand what he is reading!*

Here is an easy reading selection along with its comprehension questions:

The United States Mint has given our nation a new and interesting coin. The new coin honors Susan B. Anthony. The Mint is making millions of these "mini-dollars."

Why did Miss Anthony become the first woman to appear on a U.S. coin? Born in 1820, Susan B. Anthony devoted her life to fighting for Equality. She is most famous for helping women to gain the right to vote.

The new dollar is very unusual. It has eleven sides, and is just slightly larger than a quarter. That makes this dollar coin even smaller than the current 50 cent piece!

1. This selection is mainly about
   a) the U.S. Mint
   b) Susan B. Anthony
   c) our new dollar
   d) a fight for Equality

2. The word gain in this story means
   a) raise
   b) get
   c) grab
   d) grow

3. The new coin has been called the "mini-dollar" because of its
   a) low cost
   b) short sides
   c) small size
   d) unusual shape

4. From this selection you can tell that the U.S. Mint's job is to:
   a) make coins
   b) honor famous Americans
   c) save coins
   d) help people vote

Answers: 1. c   2. b   3. c   4. a

The reading selections also become harder to understand as the test progresses. Each reading passage is longer and includes more difficult vocabulary words than the previous selection.

This is an example of a difficult reading selection and questions:

Man's desire to exchange news began back in the Stone Age when friendly tribesmen stopped to gossip before bartering their wares. The early Colonials in America weren't much better off. They got their foreign news from tipsters, letters from friends in England, writers, travelers and visiting **dignitaries.** Month-old newspapers brought by ship from London were displayed on tavern walls.

It was Julius Caesar, author of the famous line "All Gaul is divided into three parts," who is credited with printing the first daily newspapers. He was also the first crusading journalist, taking on that role shortly after he became consul in 60 B.C. He had published Acta Diurna, or the The Daily Acts, to try to change the **crooked** politics of the time and to see that the Senate carried out no secret acts which would interfere with his own plans. These daily notices were printed on a whitened wooden board called album (white) which people would line up to read at the Forum.

from "The Trenchcoat Brigade," by United Press International

1. The best title for this selection is
   a) The Golden Age of News Reporting
   b) Julius Caesar, Crusading Journalist
   c) Man's Desire for News
   d) Ancient Rome and Colonial America

2. The writer calls early American settlers
   a) tipsters   c) writers
   b) world travelers   d) Colonials

3. The visiting **dignitaries** who brought news were
   a) clergymen   c) tourists
   b) statesmen   d) mercenaries

4. The reader learns from this selection that ancient Rome and Colonial America both had
   a) bartering for wares   c) written news
   b) a senate   d) daily newspapers

5. In this selection, the word **crooked** means
   a) dishonorable   c) careless
   b) twisted   d) wicked

6. One can conclude that the foreign news received in America was most likely:
   a) amazingly accurate   c) very up-to-date
   b) eagerly read   d) only about England

Answers: 1. c   2. d   3. b   4. c   5. a   6. b

You can see that a good vocabulary is a real asset on a reading comprehension test. *A good vocabulary enables a child to recognize the key words in the paragraphs and to understand what he reads.*

This part of the test even includes some special questions about vocabulary words in the selections. (See question #2 for the first selection, and questions #3 and 5 after the second selection.)

The children's test papers are usually sent out of the school to be marked by a computer. After a few weeks or months, the school receives the rest results. Teachers then attach the score reports to each child's permanent record for future reference.

Reading tests are generally given once a year, and good results are crucial! A low score can interfere with a child's chances for school success.

21

Helping your child develop his vocabulary knowledge is the best way to help him score high on reading tests and do well in school. A vocabulary-building program will help insure your child's chances for school success, while proving that reading is fun too!

A low reading score will hurt a child's chances for school success.

4

How To Begin
A Vocabulary-
Building Program

Your child will develop a powerful vocabulary and become a better reader as a result of following the program described in this book. With a little help from you, your child will discover and learn new vocabulary words from a variety of enjoyable materials.

Beginning the program is an exciting, special occasion. Give your child a gift assortment of books. Be sure that this **STARTER KIT** includes books which will be very appealing to your child, for they will be a pleasure to use.

Give your child a gift assortment of books.

Be careful in making your selection. Choose books which your child can read comfortably on his own. Avoid books that contain many unfamiliar vocabulary words. Too many difficult words will frustrate your child.

The STARTER KIT should include a:
- novel or book of stories (fiction)
- book about real people or events (non-fiction)
- vocabulary workbook
- word puzzle book
- dictionary
- spiral notebook

As your child finishes these books, you should replace them with other, equally enjoyable new books. A list of books that are popular with young readers begins on p.58.

Here, for example, is a sample STARTER KIT that most children in junior high school would find appealing. Recommended Kits for children in grades 3–6, can be found on pages 31 to 33.

novel:
E.T. The Extra-Terrestrial by William Kotzwinkle (Berkley)

A magical story of friendship between a ten-year-old boy and a gentle being from another world who is stranded on Earth.

non-fiction:
Encyclopedia of Amazing But True Facts by Doug Storer (Signet)

This book explores incredible and strange marvels from every corner of the Earth. These fantastic facts also prove that truth is often stranger than fiction!

vocabulary workbook:
504 Absolutely Essential Words
by Murray Bromberg, Julius Lieb, and Arthur Traiger (Barron's Educational Series)

There are 42 fast-moving lessons that teach the reader to understand and use new words through practice exercises.

word puzzle book:
The Wuzzle Book
by David Gantz (Wanderer Books)

This word puzzle ("wuzzle") book contains an exciting collection of crossword puzzles, riddles, scrambled words, cartoons, and jokes.

dictionary:
The Merriam-Webster Dictionary (Wallaby Books)
This paperback edition features large, easy-to-read type and over 57,000 entries.

spiral notebook:
Select an attractive one with 80 or 100 wide-lined pages.

(*REMINDER:* You will find STARTER KITS for other age groups on pages 31 to 33.)

HOW THE STARTER KIT SHOULD BE USED

Your child will learn many new words from the STARTER KIT. These books, and their replacements, should be used in the following ways:

Novels or Short Stories (Fiction)

Children love to read stories about the lives and adventures of others. Fiction is grouped into such categories as science fiction, mysteries, adolescent problems, sports, and romance. Select books from the category which appeals to your child the most.

Reading exciting stories is a great way to learn new vocabulary words. Here is the way your child should do it:

1. Let your child decide how many new vocabulary words to find in each book. (A realistic goal is five or ten words for each chapter.)
2. Have your child circle each new word that he comes across and wants to learn more about. (A yellow marking pen may be used instead to highlight these words.)

3. When he finishes a chapter, he should copy all the circled words into his notebook, and use the dictionary or ask you for the meanings of these words.

Let's assume that your child reads this passage in *E.T. The Extra-Terrestrial,* and is unsure about the meaning of the word "light-years":

The creature stood in the grass, his heart-light flashing with fear.

He was alone, three million (light-years) from home.

Circling "light-years" gives the word importance and makes it easy to find it again.

After reading the chapter, your child would ask you the meaning of "light-years" or look it up in the dictionary. He would then enter the meaning in the spiral notebook.

New words and their meanings are entered in the spiral notebook.

Your child would then write down all the other circled words and their meanings in the notebook. *E.T.* contains fifteen chapters. If your child circles only five new words in each chapter, he can learn 65 new vocabulary words from this book alone! If your child finds the word meanings on his own, have him pronounce the circled words for you. You might then discuss what each word means in the story.

AN OPTIONAL ACTIVITY: If your child is very enthusiastic, encourage him to use the new words in his own sentences in the notebook. You should check these sentences when he finishes to see that the words have been used correctly.

True Stories (Non-Fiction)

Children enjoy reading non-fiction books to learn more about real people, places, and things. There are books in this category to match any child's special interests. You can find biographies of famous people, books about UFO's, animals, craft ideas, cooking, and developing sports skills.

Your child would use *Amazing But True Facts* to build his vocabulary in the same way *E.T.* was used. Your child should:

1. circle the new words in each chapter;
2. enter the new words along with their meanings in the notebook;
3. discuss the word meanings with you;
4. write sentences containing these words (optional)

The first section of *Amazing But True Facts* contains many new words your child would circle and learn:

swerve	biplane	intricate
catapulted	replica	longevity
geyser	rift	hibernation
pensive	aborigine	gyroscope

IMPORTANT: It is not necessary for your child to look up every new word he finds! This practice will slow down his reading and discourage him. He should decide how many words he will find before he begins reading, and not exceed that number. Remember that your basic goal is to have your child enjoy what he reads.

Workbooks

Vocabulary workbooks are a real help in vocabulary-building. They focus on key words which frequently appear on reading tests.

Make sure that your child understands how each workbook is to be used:

1. Go over the directions for each activity.
2. Show him where to put his answers.
3. Show him how to check his answers with the correct ones in the workbook's answer section (if one is provided).
4. Tell him that you will check any sentences he may be asked to write containing the new words. (Workbooks do not supply answers for this type of exercise.)

A child who uses *504 Absolutely Essential Words,* the recommended workbook, learns to use these twelve words in Lesson 1:

abandon	tact	hardship	unaccustomed
keen	oath	gallant	bachelor
jealous	vacant	data	qualify

This workbook uses the same format in all forty-two lessons. The child reads sample sentences and a story which contains the twelve featured words. Then he must use the words himself. First he chooses which new word is missing from each of twelve practice sentences. Then he makes up his own sentences for each of the new words.

Word Puzzle Books

Children of all ages like to do word-search games and cross-word puzzles. Word games are fun to do, and provide an excellent source of new words.

Explain how each puzzle book is to be used:

1. Go over the directions together for each puzzle book.
2. Have him check his answers with the correct ones given in the book.
3. Tell him to show you his finished work. Help your child understand the words which confuse him. Use the dictionary if necessary.
4. Have him write down any words and meanings he wants to remember in his notebook.

The variety of puzzles in *The Wuzzle Book* provides many opportunities for your child to learn new words. Let's suppose that he turns to the first puzzle in the "Cross-Quiz" section of the book. The goal here is to use cartoon and crossword clues to find the missing letters that make up a mystery word.

Here are some challenging words your child will find while working on this puzzle:

residence	monarchy	observation
regal	sovereign	pertaining to

SOME HELPFUL HINTS

Remind your child that some of the new words he finds in his reading will actually look like words he already knows. Familiar-looking words can sometimes have a variety of meanings depending upon how they are used. For example, notice how the word "settle" has a different meaning in each of the following sentences:

a) The Mormons *settled* in Utah. (moved to a new place)
b) Serious disputes are often *settled* in court. (decided)

29

c) Why does the chocolate always *settle* to the bottom of the glass? (sink)

Your child should work on the program in an organized, efficient way. Set up a schedule before starting the program. Your child might begin by spending as little as fifteen to thirty minutes a day on the program. Let him increase this work time when he is ready. Encourage your child to set realistic goals for himself. You do not want him to lose interest from overwork.

Make sure that your child can work on the program without interruptions. The time set aside for reading should not conflict with dinner time or his favorite TV programs. You should be available to answer any questions, and to check over his work when he finishes it.

Have your child keep a daily record of work completed in the back of the spiral notebook. This practice will help your child keep track of his work and also give him a sense of accomplishment. Work done should be recorded in this way:

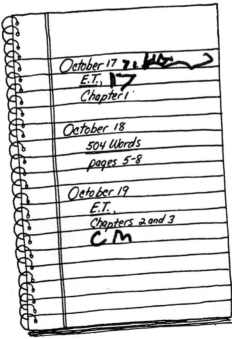

Work completed is entered in the back of the notebook.

STARTER KITS FOR OTHER AGE GROUPS

The following STARTER KIT is recommended for children in grades 3 and 4:

novel:
Tales of a Fourth Grade Nothing by Judy Blume (Dell)
Peter's parents are always after him to control his pesky two-year-old brother Fudge. When Fudge gets at Peter's pet turtle, it's just the last straw!

non-fiction:
Encyclopedia Brown's Second Record Book of Weird and Wonderful Facts by Donald J. Sobol (Bantam)
On which day of the week do more colds begin? What animals need 14 hours of sleep out of every 24? These questions and many more are answered in this book of funny stories, amazing facts, and little-known facts.

vocabulary workbook:
Building Word Power by Alvin Kravitz and Dan Dramer (Modern Curriculum Press)
This colorful workbook series makes learning new words fun. Each exciting lesson has either a puzzle to work, a story to read, or answers to find. (Use *Book C* for a child in the third grade, or *Book D* for a child in the fourth grade.)

word puzzle book:
Charlie Brown All-Sports Crossword Puzzles (Scholastic)
The Peanuts' characters present entertaining and appealing crossword puzzles that make learning fun for younger readers.

dictionary:
New Scholastic Dictionary of American English (Scholastic)
This dictionary contains over 40,000 vocabulary entries and more than 1,400 illustrations. Its large, easy-to-use size is perfect for readers in elementary school.

Be sure that your child understands how to use each book.

This STARTER KIT is recommended for children in grades
5 and 6:

novel:

Charlie and the Chocolate Factory by Roald Dahl (Bantam
Books)

Mr. Willy Wonka's famous chocolate factory is visited by
Charlie (the hero), and four nasty children. This is the
wonderful story of their funny and wild adventure.

non-fiction:

Ripley's Believe It or Not!
30th SERIES (Pocket Books)

The famous Ripley team explores incredible and strange
marvels from every corner of the earth.

vocabulary workbook:

Building Word Power by Alvin Kravitz and Dan Dramer (Modern Curriculum Press)

Use *Book E* for a child in the fifth grade, or *Book F* for a child in the sixth grade. (These workbooks are described in the STARTER KIT for third and fourth graders.)

word puzzle book:

Super Puzzle Challenge (Scholastic)

This activity book contains an exciting collection of word finds, crosswords, and creative activities for hours of puzzle fun.

dictionary:

New Scholastic Dictionary of American English (Scholastic)

(This dictionary is described in the STARTER kit for third and fourth graders.)

All of the STARTER KIT books described in this chapter are available directly from Learning House by using the order form in the back of this book. If your edition of the book does not have an order form, you can send for one by writing to Super Books, Box 98, Old Westbury, New York 11568.

5

How To Make Your Program A Success

Be enthusiastic about the program. Trust that it will work. Your child will share your confidence and pick up your enthusiasm. Your encouragement and support will make this special program seem worthwhile and fun to do.

Here are some successful teaching techniques used by professionals. Each one motivates children to learn:

1. Give praise for good work. Always let your child know how proud you are of his accomplishments. Have other family members do the same. If you stop caring, your child will lose interest too!

2. Encourage your child to ask you for help. Cheerfully give him your attention when he does come to you.

3. Suggest that your child save the most enjoyable activities for the end of a reading session (just like saving dessert for after dinner!)

4. Be flexible. Allow your child freedom to choose his own reading materials each day. Your child will learn new words from whatever he reads in the program!

5. Take a break from the program on weekends. Both of you will welcome a change of pace.

6. Ask your child to tell you which books he wants to read next. Exciting new books are a great reward for finishing the ones that he is presently reading.

Good teachers are sensitive to children's needs and moods. They know that it is important to work with students in a cooperative way. Avoid making the following mistakes with your child. These actions will damage everything you are trying to accomplish:

1. Never criticize your child for being stupid or lazy. Take a positive approach and you will encourage better performance.
2. Don't neglect your child when he comes to you for help. If you are unsure about an answer, promise to find the answer as soon as possible.
3. Don't be confused about what you expect your child to do. Before you give your child any new materials, look them over to understand how they are to be used.
4. Don't put too much pressure on your child. He is not a robot and must work at his own individual pace.
5. Don't take setbacks personally. You are bound to be emotionally involved in this project, but you should try to avoid showing frustration or anger. Remember that "Rome wasn't built in a day."

Direct all your efforts into making the program enjoyable for your child. This positive approach will increase the effectiveness of your program.

Your help can make all the difference.

6

How To
Measure Your
Child's Progress

Is your vocabulary-building program a success? Use the following guidelines to measure your child's progress.

Test Scores

Have your child's scores on vocabulary and reading tests significantly improved?

Scores on these tests should go up considerably even in a short period of time. For example, after working on the program for one year, your child might advance two or three years in reading ability. Scores like these would show that your child's ability increased two or three times faster than would be expected!

There is a way you can find out exactly how fast your child is becoming a better reader. Your child's guidance counselor at school will be able to help you get this information.

Ask the guidance counselor to give your child a reading test (with vocabulary and reading comprehension sections) before you start your program. Arrange for your child to be re-tested in about six months with a different "form" (or version) of the first test.

You will get the most clear and accurate picture of your child's reading progress by comparing these "before" and "after" scores. A substantial improvement (twelve to eighteen months in six months' time) is proof that your program is having a tremendous effect.

Reading Habits

Have your child's reading habits changed as a result of the program?

The program directs your child to find new words while reading. However, the real measure of success is whether your child develops an interest in reading for his own enjoyment. He should not read just to satisfy you!

Work and Study Habits

Have your child's work and study habits improved?

The program encourages him to work in an organized, efficient way. He should begin to do his assignments from school in the same conscientious manner.

Report Card Marks

Have your child's marks gone up?

As your child becomes a better reader, his marks should also improve. High marks in English, social studies, and science indicate that a child reads well.

Self-Image

Has there been a change in your child's feelings about himself?

As his reading ability and schoolwork improve, he should think more highly of himself, and appear to be a happier, more confident child.

The program described in this book can make your life more pleasurable and rewarding too! You will be thrilled to watch your child improve and become a better reader under your direction. You will have the satisfaction of knowing that *your help* made all the difference.

You will also gain satisfaction in knowing that you strengthened your relationship with your child. The program is a wonderful project that you can work on together. Your child will never forget this special time. It will stand out not only as a productive learning experience, but also as a shining example of your concern for his development and well-being.

The program is a wonderful project you can work on together.

7

More Ways
To Build
Vocabulary

As you begin to help your child become a better reader, you will begin to see everyday things in a new way. Both you and your child will quickly discover that new words are everywhere! The following section will show you how to take advantage of everyday experiences to develop your child's vocabulary.

Many printed materials come into your home on a daily basis. These common household items such as cereal boxes, mail-order catalogs, television listings, record album covers, newspapers, and magazines all contain new words that your child can learn. Encourage your child to read these materials and discuss the new words that he finds with you.

How does a child learn new words from a cereal box? Let's look at the back of a Quaker Instant Oatmeal box which appears on page 42. If your child would read this cartoon story during breakfast, he would come across these challenging words:

cautious	caution
lacked	(a Maple and Brown Sugar) buff
bolder	adventurer's club

He could learn their meanings from other family members seated around the breakfast table.

The back panel from a Quaker Instant Oatmeal cereal box.

42

Newspapers and Magazines

Your child can substantially increase his vocabulary by reading newspapers. Daily newspapers offer something for everyone. There are news stories, special features, comic strips, articles about family living, sports and entertainment sections. Encourage your child to read his favorite section of the newspaper on a regular basis. Help him to pronounce and understand any difficult words he comes across.

Children love to read magazines that are colorful and entertaining. Interesting magazine articles can also provide an excellent supply of new vocabulary words. You should consider subscribing to magazines which appeal to your child. Select those magazines that he can read easily. (A complete list of popular magazines for children and teenagers begins on page 93.)

You can also include high-interest magazines as a regular feature of your vocabulary-building program. Your child would use them in the same way he uses the fiction and non-fiction books in the STARTER KIT. He would:

1. schedule magazine reading as part of his usual vocabulary-building time;
2. circle the new words in each article;
3. enter these words along with their meanings in the spiral notebook;
4. discuss the word meanings with you;
5. write sentences containing these words (optional).

Scrapbooks

Did you ever start a scrapbook? Do you remember how much fun it was? Your child would probably enjoy keeping one for a favorite team, TV star, hobby or other special interest. He can start a scrapbook by mounting appropriate newspaper clippings or magazine articles on unlined or construction paper. Your child will be eager to look through magazines and newspapers to find more items to add to the scrapbook.

(As an optional activity here, your child could circle the new words in the articles, and write their meanings in the scrapbook too.)

Comic Books

Comic books have a tremendous appeal to young readers. Your child can learn many valuable new words from wholesome comics, for they are educational as well as entertaining. Your child should learn the meanings of the new words he comes across in comics by asking you or using the dictionary. He can keep a list of the words and meanings he finds in the spiral notebook.

The first page of a cartoon story from an *Archie at Riverdale High* comic book appears on page 45. The rest of the story tells how Archie eventually finds a way to stop Scoop Scanlon from printing sensational headlines in the school newspaper. The action on that page shows the powerful effect one word can have in a newspaper headline.

Young readers learn from this story that responsible newspapers carefully compose their headlines to avoid distorting the truth. Readers clearly see how two very similar words can have completely different meanings: *visiting* a jail is very different from *going to* jail!

A child who reads this comic book also has the opportunity to learn three newspaper-related terms from this page alone:

scandal sheet   scoop   libelous

Games

Your child can have fun building his vocabulary by playing educational games with a friend or a member of the family. Consider buying any of these popular and worthwhile games for your child's education and enjoyment:

ALPHABET SOUP (age 4 to 8) Each player draws alphabet letters to spell the names of animals pictured on the game board. (Parker Brothers)

A page from an Archie at Riverdale High *comic book.*

BOGGLE (age 8 and up) Players must make words from 16 lettered cubes. Each player must race against time and his opponents. (Parker Brothers)

FAMILY FEUD (age 10 and up) *Family Feud* is based on the popular TV game show. Players form teams and take turns in trying to answer challenging questions. (Milton Bradley)

GO TO THE HEAD OF THE CLASS (age 8 and up) Players move ahead from desk to desk when they correctly answer general information questions. (Milton Bradley Games)

PASSWORD (age 10 and up) Players help their teammates guess secret words by supplying clues. (Milton Bradley Games)

PEOPLE – THE TRIVIA GAME (age 12 and up) Which U.S. President was once a football broadcaster? The answer to that question and thousands more are here in this trivia game adapted from *People Magazine*. (Parker Brothers)

PERQUACKEY (age 8 and up) Players use letter cubes to form as many words as the timer allows. (Lakeside Games)

RAZZLE (age 8 and up) This word game is played on a mechanical "football field." Players win points by finding hidden words and moving towards the opponent's goal line. (Parker Brothers)

SCRABBLE (age 8 and up) The object of this crossword game is to use letter tiles to form words on the game board. (Selchow & Righter)

SCRABBLE ALPHABET GAME (age 4 to 6) Preschoolers can learn their ABC's while playing this game with three-dimensional alphabet letters. (Selchow & Righter)

SCRABBLE CROSSWORD CUBES (age 8 and up) Players form words in crossword fashion with letter cubes, while racing against a timer. (Selchow & Righter)

SCRABBLE CROSSWORD GAME FOR JUNIORS (ages 6 to 10) Here is a crossword game designed for younger children. (Selchow & Righter)

TRIVIAL PURSUIT (age 7 and up) The Young Players Edition of this popular game provides hours of fun with 6,000 intriguing trivia questions. (Selchow & Righter)

Educational games offer an enjoyable way to learn new words.

UPWORDS (age 10 and up) The object of this 3-dimensional game is to build words across, down, and upwards with stackable letter tiles. (Milton Bradley)

WHEEL OF FORTUNE (age 10 and up) In this fast-action word game based upon the popular TV game show, each player competes to solve a phrase hidden on the puzzle board. (Pressman)

Television and Radio

Your child can add many new words to his vocabulary by listening more carefully to television and radio programs. Encourage your child to ask a family member for help in understanding new words he hears during shows, news reports, and even commercials. You can also ask him whether he knows the meanings of words you hear together on the TV or radio.

Advertising

Most advertisements contain rich and colorful words which describe a product or service. Encourage your child to read highway billboards, posters on buses and trains, and advertising displays in stores. These advertisements are an excellent source of new words you can discuss with your child.

Sales brochures for new automobiles are an especially worth-while form of advertising because they can introduce your child to many new words. These booklets make exciting reading for young car enthusiasts, and they are easy to obtain at new car dealerships.

Here is a section from a recent Chevrolet Camaro brochure:

Camaro interiors

Slip into Camaro's roomy cockpit-style interior and you know you're in for some very special road action.

Those handsomely sculpted, full-foam bucket seats are shaped to help provide comfort on long trips and short jaunts.

That precisely placed instrument cluster is there to update you on performance data. The newly designed instrument panel pad and gage cluster bezel have a striking visual effect.

And there is luxury. Luxury in the

wall-to-wall cut-pile carpeting, artfully tailored upholstery and in the custom-blended interior color schemes.

Now, choose your interior colors and materials. But do it with care. Both you and your new Camaro deserve it.

Sales brochures for new automobiles are exciting to read.

From this vivid description, a child could learn the meanings of these words:

interior	precisely	artfully-tailored upholstery
sculpted	update	custom-blended color schemes
jaunts	gauge cluster	

Souvenirs

When you take your child to see a special event, such as the circus or a professional ball game, buy a souvenir booklet if one is available. Your child will enjoy reading it, and he will also have an opportunity to learn new words.

Try to find interesting materials for your child to read when you take vacation trips. A visitor to the United Nation's gift shop in New York City would find a variety of appealing gifts for children. One delightful item sold there is a cookbook entitled *MANY HANDS COOKING: An International Cookbook for Girls and Boys.*

This cookbook features forty recipes from around the world that children can prepare. Here is one recipe from this cookbook.

From
SWEDEN
MEAT BALLS
Serves 4 ♦♦♦

The original meaning of the word *smorgasbord* was sandwich board. Long ago the Vikings used a flat piece of bread as a plate and piled their other foods on top of it. Today a smorgasbord is a buffet.

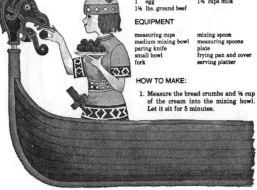

The table is set with many different kinds of hot and cold foods. Swedes have a special order for arranging them: dishes of cold fish first; then cold meat; next, small hot dishes (such as these Meat Balls); and finally dessert. The foods you select are piled on a plate, but bread is still a must on the table.

You don't need to have a smorgasbord to enjoy these Meat Balls. They make a delightful dish for lunch, dinner, or Sunday brunch.

INGREDIENTS

¾ cup bread crumbs	2 t. salt
1 cup cream	¼ t. ground allspice
1 onion	2 T. butter
1 egg	2 T. flour
1¼ lbs. ground beef	1½ cups milk

EQUIPMENT

measuring cups	mixing spoon
medium mixing bowl	measuring spoons
paring knife	plate
small bowl	frying pan and cover
fork	serving platter

HOW TO MAKE:

1. Measure the bread crumbs and ½ cup of the cream into the mixing bowl. Let it sit for 5 minutes.
2. With the paring knife, peel the onion and chop it up into small pieces.
3. Break the egg into the small bowl and beat it with the fork.
4. Add the meat and the cut-up onion to the bread crumbs and cream. Mix well.
5. Stir in the egg, the salt, and the allspice.
6. Pick up a small amount of the mixture—about as big as a plum—with your hand. Roll it between your palms. Shape it into a ball. Place each ball when you have made it on the plate. Continue until all the meat is rolled into balls.
7. Melt the butter in the frying pan, over low heat.
8. Place a few meat balls in the pan. Roll them from side to side with the spoon till they are browned on all sides. Remove them to a plate. Continue until all the balls are browned. Turn off the heat.
9. Add the flour to the frying pan. Stir it with the fat and meat juice until it is all mixed together. Scrape up the meat that has stuck to the bottom of the pan with the mixing spoon.
10. Add the second ½ cup of cream and the milk to the mixture in the pan. Stir it until it makes a smooth sauce.
11. Return the meat balls to the frying pan with the sauce. Cover the pan with a lid.
12. Simmer it over a very low flame for 25 minutes.
13. Arrange the meat balls on the serving platter and pour the gravy over them.

A recipe from MANY HANDS COOKING: An International Cookbook for Girls and Boys (UNICEF)

A child could learn these new words while learning how to prepare Swedish meat balls:

smorgasbord	buffet	paring knife
Vikings	brunch	simmer

This exceptional cookbook also features a special glossary of kitchen terms which can help build vocabulary.

(You can order this cookbook by writing to the United States Committee for UNICEF, 331 East 38th Street, New York, N.Y. 10016.)

Encourage your child to learn new words from every available source. Remember that wherever you are, there are many opportunities for your child to learn new words. Help him make the most of these opportunities, and you will help your child to become a super reader!

8

Good Books
For Young
Readers

The first part of this chapter lists books which will bring hours of reading enjoyment to preschoolers and children in the early elementary grades. These picture books are ideal for reading aloud with your young son or daughter. With your help, your child will share adventures with storybook characters, delight in the amusing pictures, and learn to recognize many basic words.

The other sections in this chapter organize books into the same categories as in the STARTER KITS which were described on pages 24 to 33. These groupings will make it easy for you to select additional books to use in your vocabulary-building program. The approximate grade level and interest appeal are also indicated for each book or series of books. Even if you decide not to begin the program at home, you can use these listings to find some of the very best books available for young people in grades 3–9.

Almost all of the books in this chapter are available in inexpensive, paperback editions. When a title is also available in a hardcover edition, the paperback publisher's name will appear first as in "Dell/Bradbury Press."

Most of these books are available in local bookstores. If certain titles are difficult to find, you can order them directly from the publishers. A list of publisher's addresses is included at the end of the section.

To find additional good books for young readers, some helpful guides are listed in the Appendix under "More Recommended Reading Lists for Children."

FIRST BOOKS

AMELIA BEDELIA by Peggy Parish

Amelia Bedelia is everybody's favorite nut! Some very wacky things happen when this housemaid starts turning things upside-down. Amelia's adventures continue in *Come Back, Amelia Bedelia, Play Ball, Amelia Bedelia,* and *Teach Us, Amelia Bedelia.* (Scholastic/Harper)

BEDTIME FOR FRANCIS by Russel Hoban

Frances, a badger, tries every trick to stay up past bedtime. (Harper)

BERENSTAIN BEAR BOOKS by Stan and Jan Berenstain

The adorable family of Berenstain Bears has wonderful adventures together in *The Bear Scouts, The Bears' Picnic, The Bears' Vacation, The Berenstain Bears' Moving Day, The Bike Lesson,* and many other fun books. (Random House)

BIG BEAR SPARE THAT TREE by Richard Margolis

The heartwarming story of a blue jay who tries to convince Big Bear not to chop down the tree where she has built her nest. (Scholastic)

BRUNUS AND THE NEW BEAR by Ellen Stoll Walsh

Brunus has been Benjamin's favorite stuffed bear for many years. When Benjamin gets a stuffed baby bear and forgets about Brunus — Brunus doesn't like it! (Field/Doubleday)

THE CARROT SEED by Ruth Krauss

A little boy plants a carrot seed which no one thinks will grow— but he knows better! (Harper)

CLIFFORD THE BIG RED DOG by Norman Bridwell

The very funny story of Elizabeth's giant dog, Clifford. Also available: *Clifford Gets a Job, Clifford Takes a Trip,* and *Clifford the Small Red Puppy.* (Scholastic)

A CHICK HATCHES by Joanna Cole

Exciting step-by-step photographs detail the miracle of a chick growing inside an egg. (Morrow)

CURIOUS GEORGE by H.A. Rey

Curious George tries to find out about everything and always gets himself into big trouble! The little monkey continues his mischief in *Curious George Gets a Medal, Curious George Learns the Alphabet,* and *Curious George Takes a Job.* (Houghton Mifflin)

DR. SEUSS BOOKS

Children and parents delight in Dr. Seuss' unforgettable stories, clever rhymes, and zany drawings. Titles available include *Bartholomew and the Oobleck, Cat in the Hat, Green Eggs and Ham, Horton Hatches the Egg, On Beyond Zebra,* and *Scrambled Eggs Super.* (Random House)

GEORGE AND MARTHA by James Marshall

Two friendly hippos teach each other what caring, sharing, and friendship are all about. George and Martha's adventures continue in *George and Martha Encore, George and Martha One Fine Day,* and *George and Martha Rise and Shine.* (Houghton Mifflin)

GOODNIGHT MOON by Margaret Wise Brown

The story of a little rabbit who prepares for bed and says goodnight to all the things in his room. (Harper)

HARRY THE DIRTY DOG by Gene Zion

Harry the dog gets himself so dirty that even his own family doesn't recognize him! (Harper)

THE HOUSE ON EAST 88TH STREET by Bernard Waber

When the Primm family moves into their new house they find a large, green crocodile in their bathtub! The humorous adventures of Lyle the lovable crocodile continue in *Lyle and the Birthday Party, Lovable Lyle, Lyle Finds His Mother,* and *Lyle, Lyle, Crocodile.* (Houghton Mifflin)

IRA SLEEPS OVER by Bernard Waber

Ira wants to sleep over at his friend Reggie's house, but he has never spent a night without his teddy bear before. (Houghton Mifflin)

LITTLE GOLDEN BOOKS

Little Golden Books have been the favorite first books of children for many years. Outstanding titles in the series include *Bambi, Cinderella, A Day on the Farm, Donald Duck's Toy Train, Frosty the Snowman, Mickey Mouse's Picnic,* and *The Little Red Caboose.* (Golden)

LITTLE TOOT by Hardie Gramatky

Toot the Tugboat learns to take responsibility and become a hero. (Putnam)

MADELEINE by Ludwig Bemelmans

This popular classic tells about the adventures of a French schoolgirl and her 11 friends in Paris. Madeleine and her classmates' adventures continue in *Madeleine and the Gypsies, Madeleine in London,* and *Madeleine's Rescue.* (Puffin)

MAKE WAY FOR DUCKLINGS by Robert McCloskey

Mr. and Mrs. Mallard travel through the busy streets of Boston looking for the perfect spot to raise their family. (Puffin/Viking)

MIKE MULLIGAN AND HIS STEAM SHOVEL by Virginia Burton

Mary Anne, the steam shovel, is old-fashioned, but she and her owner prove they can finish a big job for the town of Popperville. (Houghton Mifflin)

MORRIS THE MOOSE GOES TO SCHOOL by B. Wiseman

The hilarious mishaps of a lovable moose who wants to learn to read and count. (Scholarship/Harper)

PAT THE BUNNY by Dorothy Kunhardt

This children's classic has a soft felt bunny for preschoolers to pat, a Daddy's scratchy face to feel, and other surprises to spark a tot's curiosity. (Golden)

PICTURE-BOARD BOOKS

These sturdy, full-color picture books of toys, animals, foods, and numbers are perfect for toddlers. Many series are available including *Chubby Board Books* (Wanderer), *Little Simon Puppet Story Books* (Simon & Schuster) and, *Teddy Board Books* (Platt & Munk).

RANDOM HOUSE PICTUREBACK SERIES

This series offers 64 paperbacks with strong appeal to young children. Titles that are sure to become favorites are *Animal Babies, Babar Learns to Cook, The Berenstain Bears' New Baby, Big Joe's Trailer Truck,* and *Farm Animals.* (Random House)

RICHARD SCARRY BOOKS

These first books for young children are a wonderful introduction to reading about places and things in a child's everyday world. Friendly animals explore the zoo, the supermarket, the circus, school, weather, numbers, flowers, toys, and more. Titles include *All Day Long, Animal Nursery Tales, Cars and Trucks and Things That Go, My House, On Vacation, Richard Scarry's Best First Book Ever,* and *Richard Scarry's Best Word Book Ever.* (Golden/Random House)

SESAME STREET BOOKS

The lovable Muppets from the celebrated TV show present numbers, letters, shapes, and delightful stories. The world of "Sesame Street" books includes *Big Bird's Busy Book, The Sesame Street ABC Storybook, The Sesame Street Bedtime Storybook, The Sesame Street Little Library, The Sesame Street Storybook,* and many more. (Golden/Random House)

SMALL PIG by Arnold Lobel

The funny adventures of a small pig who goes in search of nice squishy mud. (Harper)

THE SNOWY DAY by Ezra Jack Keats

An enchanting tale about a day a little boy spends during a snowy day in the city. Also by the author: *Dreams, Goggles!, Louie, Pet Show!, The Trip,* and *Whistle for Willie.* (Puffin/ Viking)

THE STORY OF BABAR by Jean De Brunhoff

The first in a series of stories about Babar, the elephant-king who leaves home in search of adventure. Many more humorous *Babar* titles are available. (Random House)

THE STORY OF PING by Marjorie Flack

In a story of life on the Yangtse River in the China of long ago, Ping, a mischievious duck, narrowly escapes becoming somebody's supper. (Puffin/Viking)

SYLVESTER AND THE MAGIC PEBBLE by William Steig

Sylvester, a young donkey, finds a magic pebble which grants him any wish. (Simon & Schuster)

THERE'S A NIGHTMARE IN MY CLOSET by Mercer Meyer

A young boy conquers his fear of the dark and of the strange creatures hovering there. (Field/Dial)

THUNDERHOOF by Syd Hoff

Thunderhoof roams the West wild and free. Then this proud horse learns he likes cowboys better than the open range. (Field/Harper)

THE VELVETEEN RABBIT by Margery Williams

Can a stuffed toy ever become "real"? Here is the wonderful, classic story of the Velveteen Rabbit who does. (Avon/Doubleday)

THE VERY HUNGRY CATERPILLAR by Eric Carle

This captivating book teaches numbers, the days of the week, and the reasons why a very hungry caterpillar can't get enough to eat. (Philomel)

WHERE THE WILD THINGS ARE by Maurice Sendak

Max's imagination takes him to the land of wild things, but he soon decides that home is the best place. (Harper)

FICTION BOOKS

THE ADVENTURES OF SHERLOCK HOLMES by Sir Arthur Conan Doyle (adapted by Catherine Edwards Sadler) (gr 4–7)

The four books in this series present 14 incredible mysteries that challenge Sherlock Holmes, the extraordinary detective, and his trusted friend, Dr. Watson. (Avon)

ALDO ICE CREAM by Johanna Hurwitz (gr 3–6)

Aldo Sossi loves to sample all the new flavors at the local ice cream store. His great scheme is to earn enough money to buy his big sister an ice cream maker for her birthday! (Archway/ Morrow)

ALEXANDER AND THE TERRIBLE, HORRIBLE, NO GOOD, VERY BAD DAY by Judith Viorst (K-4)

The humorous story of how everything goes wrong for Alexander all day long, starting with gum in his hair and no prize in his cereal box. (Atheneum)

ALFRED HITCHCOCK AND THE THREE INVESTIGATORS SERIES (gr 4–7)

Three adventurous young detectives get involved in 35 thrilling mysteries filled with danger and suspense. Each book is introduced by Alfred Hitchcock. (Random House)

ALL-OF-A-KIND FAMILY by Sidney Taylor (gr 3–7)

Five daughters in a family grow up with high spirits and lots of love on New York's lower east side at the turn of the century. The warmth and humor of their day-to-day adventures are continued in *All-of-a-Kind Family Downtown* and *Ella of All-of-a-Kind Family*. (Dell)

BEST FRIENDS DON'T COME IN THREES by Joel L. Schwartz (gr 3–6)

Richie has always thought nothing could come between him and his best buddy. Is it possible for a tight twosome to become a close trio? (Dell)

BIG RED by Jim Kjelgaard (gr 7–9)

The wilderness adventure of a boy and a champion Irish setter who form an unbreakable friendship. Also by the author: *Desert Dog, Irish Red, Outlaw Red,* and *Stormy.* (Bantam)

THE BLACK STALLION BOOKS by Walter Farley (gr 4–7)

Adventure and suspense for young horse lovers in six action-packed titles. (Random House)

JUDY BLUME BOOKS (Dell/Bradbury, Dutton)

This author's books are tremendously popular with young readers because they deal with what it's really like to grow up. Each book reflects some of the joys, fears, and uncertainties of childhood and adolescence.

Are You There God? It's Me Margaret   The story of a sensitive girl on the brink of adolescence. (gr 5–8)

Blubber   Fifth grade children are cruel to a classmate because she is fat. (gr 4–6)

Deenie   Attractive Deenie is told she must wear a metal brace for a back condition. (gr 5–7)

Freckle Juice   Andrew will do anything to have freckles just like his friend Nicky. (gr 3–5)

Iggie's House   Three black children move into a white neighborhood and want friends, not just "good neighbors." (gr 4–7)

It's Not the End of the World   Karen Newman must cope with her parents' divorce. (gr 5-8)

The One in the Middle is the Green Kangaroo   Freddy, the middle kid in the family, gets a part in the school play and has a chance to show how special he really is. (K–3)

Otherwise Known as Sheila the Great   A humorous story about how Sheila Tubman learns self-confidence. (gr 4–6)

Starring Sally J. Freedman as Herself   It is 1947 and the Freedman's are happily spending the winter in Florida, but Sally can't forget the terrible war. (gr 4–7)

Superfudge   Peter Hatcher's got a problem: he's had to put up with his pesky little brother, Fudge, for four long years and now a new baby is coming! (gr 3–6)

Then Again, Maybe I Won't   13 year-old Tony Miglione has nothing but problems after his father's invention makes the family rich. (gr 3-6)

FRANK BONHAM BOOKS (gr 7-h.s.)

Frank Bonham's stories ring with the life, excitement, and toughness of the Los Angeles-Watts area. He has written many widely acclaimed books for young readers including *Durango Street, The Mystery of the Fat Cat, Viva Chicano, The Nitty Gritty,* and *Cool Cat.* (Dell)

CHOOSE YOUR OWN ADVENTURE SERIES by R. Montgomery, E. Packard, and D. Terman (gr 3—8)

Young readers have great fun with this terrific series. In each *Choose Your Own Adventure* book, the reader is the hero of the story and must often decide among many incredibly daring experiences. The best part is that each book can be read over and over again with a different surprise ending each time. Titles include *The Cave of Time, Journey Under the Sea, By Balloon to the Sahara, Space and Beyond, The Mystery of Chimney Rock,* and over fifty more stories. (Bantam)

THE CITY ROSE by Ruth White Miller (gr 6-8)

Dee Bristol must search for new roots after a tragic fire sweeps through her family's Detroit apartment. (Avon/McGraw Hill)

CLOSE ENCOUNTERS OF THE THIRD KIND by Steven Spielberg (gr 7 — h.s.)

Humans and aliens from space make unexpected, dramatic contact. (Dell)

BEVERLY CLEARY BOOKS

Children love to read about the humorous adventures of Beverly Cleary's unforgettable characters. These delightful books rank high on the list of children's all-time favorites.

Dear Mr. Henshaw Leigh Botts writes letters to his favorite author, and the answers he gets back change his life. (gr 4—6) (Dell/Morrow)

Ellen Tebbits If Ellen Tebbits had just one wish, it would be that she and Austine Allen could become best friends again. (gr 3-7) (Dell/Morrow)

Henry and Beezus Henry Huggins invents wild money-making schemes to earn a new bike, and Beezus (short for

Beatrice Quimby) volunteers to join in. (gr 3-7) (Dell/Morrow)

Henry and the Clubhouse When Henry and his friends decide to post a "No girls allowed" sign on their clubhouse, Beezus and her little sister Ramona decide they won't be kept out. (gr 3-7) (Dell/Morrow)

Jean and Johnny Jean's father doesn't want her "chasing after boys." Yet Jean is sure Johnny really likes her . . . but does he? (gr 6-9) (Scholastic/Morrow)

The Mouse and the Motorcycle Adventurous Ralph the mouse learns to ride a motorcycle in this delightful, humorous story. Ralph's story is continued in *Runaway Ralph*. (gr 3-5) (Archway/Morrow)

Ramona the Brave Ramona really tries to grow up, but she just can't seem to stay out of trouble. (gr 4-6) (Scholastic/Morrow)

Ramona and Her Father After her father loses his job, Ramona does everything she can to make her father happy again. (gr 3-7) (Dell/Morrow)

Ramona the Pest Ramona has tremendous fun becoming the biggest pest in town. (gr 3-5) (Scholastic/Morrow)

Ribsy Ribsy, Henry Huggins' dog, gets lost. As he tries to find his way home, he has one funny adventure after another. (gr 3-7) (Archway/Morrow)

Runaway Ralph After his mother decides that his shiny, mouse-sized motorcycle is unsafe, Ralph decides to run away. Danger stalks Ralph from the moment he leaves home. (gr 3-6) (Dell/Morrow)

THE CRICKET IN TIMES SQUARE by George Selden (gr 4-7)

The wonderful tale of a musical cricket from rural Connecticut who spends the summer in a New York subway befriended by a mouse, a cat, and a boy. Chester Cricket and his friends meet again in the sequels, *Tucker's Countryside* and *Chester Cricket's Pigeon Ride.* (Dell/Farrar, Straus, & Giroux)

DANNY DUNN SERIES by Jay Williams and Raymond Abrashkin (gr 4-7)

Danny, and his friends Joe and Irene, have great fun being scientific super-detectives in fifteen stories. (Archway/McGraw Hill)

PAULA DANZIGER BOOKS (Dell/Delacorte)

In an enjoyable, easy-to-read style, Paula Danziger balances the daily trauma of the young adult years with lots of humor. Her stories include:

Can You Sue Your Parents for Malpractice? Lauren Allen's life is the pits at home and at school. Yet Lauren slowly learns to make decisions that are right for her. (gr 7-h.s.)

The Cat Ate My Gymsuit Marcy Lewis decides to take a stand after Ms. Finney, her favorite teacher, gets suspended from her job. (gr 6-9)

The Divorce Express Since her parents' divorce, ninth-grader Phoebe must shuttle back and forth from weekends with Dad in the country to weekdays with Mom in the city. (gr 7-h.s.)

The Pistachio Prescription War is waged daily in Cassandra Stephens' home, beginning at the breakfast table and ending with slammed doors at night. (gr 7-h.s.)

There's a Bat in Bunk Five Marcy's thrilled to be a junior counselor at a new creative-arts camp, but camp life is anything but perfect! (gr 6–h.s.)

DEAR LOVEY HART, I AM DESPARATE by Ellen Conford (gr 7–h.s.)

Carrie decides to write the lovelorn advice column for her school newspaper and her troubles begin! (Scholastic/Little, Brown)

DINKY HOCKER SHOOTS SMACK! by M.E. Kerr (gr 7–h.s.)

Dinky, a food freak, humorously shares her problems with her friends and an overweight cat named Nader. (Dell/Harper)

THE EARS OF LOUIS by Constance C. Greene (gr 3-7)

Louis is sick and tired of people noticing his big ears and calling him names. He even starts sticking his ears to the sides of his head with Scotch tape! (Dell/Viking)

EDGAR ALLAN by John Neufeld (gr 5–8)

The deeply-moving story of a young black child adopted by a white middle-class suburban family. (Signet)

ENCYCLOPEDIA BROWN SERIES by Donald J. Sobol (gr 3–6)

Encyclopedia Brown is known as America's Sherlock Holmes in sneakers. Each book contains ten new baffling mysteries the reader is invited to solve. (Bantam, Dell, and Scholastic/Lodestar)

THE ENORMOUS EGG by Oliver Butterworth (gr 3–6)

The funny story of an enormous egg which hatches into a dinosaur. (Dell/Little, Brown)

FAT MEN FROM SPACE by Daniel M. Pinkwater (gr 3–7)

Worldwide panic sets in when thousands of fat spacemen invade Earth, confiscating and eating all the junk food they can find! (Dell/Dodd, Mead)

A FATHER EVERY FEW YEARS by Alice Bach (gr 7-h.s.)

Tim says he hates Max for walking out on his mother, but

deep down he misses his fun-loving stepfather. (Dell/Harper)

FREAKY FRIDAY by Mary Rodgers (gr 5–8)

Humorous events happen when a mother and daughter mysteriously switch places for a day. (Harper)

FROM THE MIXED-UP FILES OF MRS. BASIL E. FRANK-WEILER by E.L. Konigsburg (gr 3-7)

Claudia and her brother Jamie decide to teach their parents a lesson. The two move into the Metropolitan Museum of Art, and refuse to go home until they solve a puzzling mystery. (Dell/Atheneum)

GENTLE BEN by Walt Morey (gr 5–9)

A moving story of friendship between a 13-year-old boy and an Alaskan Brown bear. (Avon/Dutton)

THE GIRL WITH THE SILVER EYES by Willo Davis Roberts (gr 4–6)

Katie's ability to communicate with animals starts her on a suspense-filled search for others like herself. (Scholastic/Atheneum)

THE GREAT McGONIGGLE'S GRAY GHOST by Scott Corbett (gr 3–5)

Mac McGoniggle and his friend Ken Wetzel search through an old Victorian house for a valuable prize. (Dell/Little, Brown)

HARDY BOYS MYSTERY STORIES by Franklin W. Dixon (gr 4–8)

Young readers who like adventure stories packed with mystery and action will love this thrilling 80-book series which begins with *The Tower Treasure* and *The House on the Cliff.* (Wanderer/Grosset & Dunlap)

HARRIET THE SPY by Louise Fitzhugh (gr 3–8)

When Harriet's secret notebook about her parents and friends is discovered, the results are hilarious. (Dell/Harper)

CAROLYN HAYWOOD BOOKS (Harcourt)

Carolyn Haywood's books have a special charm for children. These stories are packed with new adventures, growing-up experiences, and just the kind of good times and scrapes children love to read about. Books in this series include *"B" Is For Betsy, Back to School with Betsy, Betsy and Billy, Betsy and the Boys, Here's a Penny,* and *Penny and Peter.* (gr 3–5)

S.E. HINTON BOOKS (gr 7–h.s.)

This popular author portrays the tough, violent side of teenage life in her best-selling novels which include *The Outsiders, That Was Then, This Is Now,* and *Rumble Fish.* (Dell/Viking)

THE HOBOKEN CHICKEN EMERGENCY by D. Manus Pinkwater (gr 3–6)

Henrietta, Arthur's pet chicken is missing somewhere in Hoboken. What's so unusual? Henrietta is 15 feet high and weighs 266 pounds! (Scholastic/Prentice-Hall)

THE HOCUS-POCUS DILEMNA by Pat Kibbe (gr 4–7)

B.J. Pinkerton is driving her family crazy with fortune-telling powers that are always right on target. B.J.'s hilarious adventures continue in *My Mother the Mayor, Maybe.* (Scholastic/Knopf)

HOMER PRICE by Robert McCloskey (gr 4–6)

Six short stories (including "The Doughnuts") describe the humorous adventures of Homer Price, Aunt Aggy, and Uncle

Ulysses. Homer's adventures are continued in *Centerburg Tales*. (Puffin/Viking)

A HORSE CALLED MYSTERY by Marjorie Reynolds (gr 3–6)

Owlie buys Mystery, a lame horse, instead of the bicycle he wanted. Together they teach the town an unforgettable lesson. (Harper)

THE HOUSE OF DIES DREAR by Virginia Hamilton (gr 6-9)

Young Thomas and his family move into a house that Dies Drear, an abolitionist, converted into a station on the underground railway. According to legend, the passageways are haunted by the ghosts of Drear and two fugitive slaves murdered there over a century ago! (Dell/Macmillan)

A HOUSE OF THIRTY CATS by Mary Calhoun (gr 4–6)

Sarah finds a way to save Miss Tabitha Henshaw's thirty wonderful cats from a spiteful neighbor. (Archway)

HOW TO EAT FRIED WORMS by Thomas Rockwell (gr 4–6)

After losing a bet, Billy must eat fifteen worms in fifteen days! (Dell/Franklin Watts)

THE INCREDIBLE JOURNEY by Sheila Burnford (gr 6–h.s.)

Three animals endure severe hardships and travel 250 miles through Canadian wilderness to find their master. (Bantam/Little, Brown)

INVASION OF THE BODY SNATCHERS by Jack Finney (gr 7–h.s.)

Space aliens silently take over a small town in California in this spine-tingling tale. (Dell)

JAWS by Peter Benchley (gr 7–h.s.)

Terror hits an ocean resort community besieged by a 20 foot man-eating shark. (Bantam/Doubleday)

THE LANCELOT CLOSES AT FIVE by Marjorie W. Sharmat (gr 4–6)

A very humorous story about two girls who hide out overnight in a model home and learn a lesson about responsibility. (Scholastic/Macmillan)

LISA, BRIGHT AND DARK by John Neufeld (gr 7–h.s.)

An emotionally-disturbed girl gets help from her friends after adults refuse to acknowledge her problems. (Signet)

LITTLE HOUSE ON THE PRAIRIE BOOKS by Laura Ingalls Wilder (Harper)

Classic stories of pioneer life in the 1880's – 1890's are re-

lated in this series.

Little House in the Big Woods The Ingalls Family lives in a cabin in Wisconsin surrounded by wolves and a lonely forest. (gr 3–7)

Little House on the Prairie Laura and her family move West in a covered wagon through Indian territory. (gr 3–7)

Farmer Boy Almanzo Wilder's interesting life on a farm in upstate New York. (gr 3–7)

On the Banks of Plum Creek The Ingalls' must cope with a blizzard and a grasshopper plague. (gr 3–7)

By the Shores of Silver Lake As Laura turns 13, Pa helps construct a railroad in the Dakota Territory. (gr 4–8)

The Long Winter Almanzo Wilder risks his life to save the village from starvation. (gr 4–8)

Little Town on the Prairie Laura, now 15, begins to teach in a frontier town. (gr 4–8)

These Happy Golden Years Laura and Almanzo marry and begin a new life. (gr 5–9)

LUDELL by Brenda Wilkinson (gr 6–9)

It's not easy growing up when you're poor. But Ludell Wilson has something special — a joy in living that helps her overcome the hardships of getting by. (Bantam/Harper)

M.C. HIGGINS, THE GREAT by Virginia Hamilton (gr 7-h.s.)

M.C. helps his family find a better life away from the dreary mines of Appalachia. (Dell/Macmillan)

MARIA LOONEY AND THE REMARKABLE ROBOT by Jerome Beatty, Jr. (gr 4-7)

Tommy Tonn the robot cooks, cleans, does homework, and never even complains. When Tommy is robotnapped, Maria tries to rescue him despite powerful odds. (Avon)

ME AND FAT GLENDA by Lila Perl (gr 3–6)

Sarah and Glenda become great friends. (Archway/Houghton)

ME AND THE TERRIBLE TWO by Ellen Conford (gr 4-6)

Dorrie is sure that life will never be the same after her best friend moves away and a pair of identical twin boys become her new neighbors (Archway/Little, Brown)

THE MEAT IN THE SANDWICH by Alice Bach (gr 3-7)

Mike becomes a star hockey player with teammate Kip Statler's help. However, the end of hockey season brings an end to the winning combination as Mike and Kip are pitted against each other. (Dell/Harper)

MISHMASH by Molly Cone (gr 3-5)

Mishmash is a huge, friendly dog who enjoys walking into people's houses uninvited, leaping into small sports cars hoping for a ride, and sleeping in a bed with his head on the pillow! (Archway/Houghton)

MISS NELSON IS MISSING! by Harry Allard and James Marshall (K–3)

When the class in room 207 learns that their teacher, Miss Nelson, will be away for a few days, they get ready to have some fun. The class changes its tune when Miss Viola Swamp — the meanest substitute imaginable — arrives. The great fun continues in *Miss Nelson Is Back.* (Scholastic/Houghton Mifflin)

MY DAD LIVES IN A DOWNTOWN HOTEL by Peggy Mann (gr 5–7)

A sensitive boy must cope with his parents' planned divorce. (Avon/Doubleday)

NANCY DREW MYSTERY STORIES by Carolyn Keene (gr 4–7)

Carolyn Keene's famous girl sleuth gets involved in over 70 baffling adventure-filled mysteries that begin with *The Secret*

of the Old Clock and *The Hidden Staircase.* (Wanderer/Grosset
& Dunlap)

NATE THE GREAT by Marjorie Weinman Sharmat (gr 2–4)

Nate is a great detective who can solve any crime and get to
the bottom of any mystery. (Dell)

NOBODY'S FAMILY IS GOING TO CHANGE by Louise Fitzhugh (gr 4-7)

Young Emma Sheridan wants to become a lawyer as soon as
possible, and her little brother is set on being a dancer like his
Uncle Dipsey. Nothing could get their parents more upset!
(Dell/Farrar)

PADDINGTON THE BEAR BOOKS by Michael Bond (gr 3–6)

Eight delightful stories about a little bear from Peru who
brings adventure and havoc into the lives of a London family.
The series begins with *A Bear Called Paddington.* (Dell/Random
House)

PEACHES by Dindga McCannon (gr 5-8)

Peaches finds that growing up in Harlem is sometimes painful
and sometimes funny, but is always full of excitement. (Dell)

PENDULUM ILLUSTRATED STORIES (gr 3–8)

This series presents classic tales of action, adventure, and suspense in comic book form. The stories include *Black Beauty, Dr. Jekyll and Mr. Hyde, Frankenstein, Treasure Island,* and *20,000 Leagues Under the Sea.* (Pendulum Press)

PIPPI LONGSTOCKING BOOKS by Astrid Lindgren (gr 3–6)

The charming, hilarious, and absurd adventures of a totally unpredictable little girl. Titles available: *Pippi Longstocking, Pippi Goes on Board, Pippi in the South Seas.* (Puffin)

PLANET OF THE APES by Pierre Boulle (gr 7–h.s.)

Space explorers come upon a sister planet of Earth ruled by apes. (Signet)

ROLL OF THUNDER, HEAR MY CRY by Mildred D. Taylor (gr 6-9)

Cassie Logan's world is turned upside-down when night riders come to terrorize her family and destroy their farm simply because they are black. (Bantam/Dial)

THE SEVENTEENTH-STREET GANG by Emily Neville (gr 5–7)

Hollis, the new kid on the block, becomes the scapegoat of the other children in the neighborhood. (Harper)

THE SIGN OF THE BEAVER by Elizabeth G. Speare (gr 5–8)

How can Matt survive alone in the Maine wilderness after the Indians who saved his life move away? (Dell/Houghton Mifflin)

STAR WARS by George Lucas (gr 7–h.s.)

Luke Skywalker saves a beautiful princess and the forces of

the Rebellion from Darth Vader's evil Death Star. (Del Rey)

THAT DOG! by Nanette Newman (gr 1–4)

When Ben's dog dies, he feels he can never love another pet until a little puppy follows him home. (Field/Crowell)

THE THING AT THE FOOT OF THE BED by Maria Leach (gr 4–6)

Here is a spine-tingling collection of scarey ghost and witch tales. (Dell)

THE TOM SWIFT SERIES by Victor Appleton II (gr 6–9)

Tom Swift's fantastic inventions take him to all corners of the world in six different adventures. (Wanderer)

THE TROUBLE WITH THIRTEEN by Betty Miles (gr 4–7)

Annie and her best friend Rachel wish they could stay twelve forever. Everything is perfect until unexpected changes test their friendship. (Avon/Knopf)

E.B. WHITE BOOKS (gr 3–6) (Harper)

This author is well-known for writing these delightful fantasies for children:

Charlotte's Web Wilbur, a lovable pig, is rescued from a cruel fate by a beautiful and intelligent spider named Charlotte.

Stuart Little An adventurous mouse-hero searches for his lost friend, the lovely bird Margalo.

The Trumpet of the Swan A swan overcomes a handicap and becomes a famous trumpet player.

WILDFIRE ROMANCE SERIES (gr 7–h.s.)

Wildfire books are best-selling young romances that have captured the heartbeat of teen America. The series includes *A Funny Girl Like Me, Dreams Can Come True, Just Sixteen, Superflirt,* and *That's My Girl.* (Scholastic)

THE WITCH OF BLACKBIRD POND by Elizabeth G. Speare (gr 6–9)

This is the spellbinding tale of a girl who rebels against bigotry in a Puritan colony by befriending a woman accused of witchcraft. (Dell/Houghton Mifflin)

YOBGORGLE: MYSTERY MONSTER OF LAKE ONTARIO
by Daniel M. Pinkwater (gr 3–6)

Eugene Winkleman has the craziest, strangest, and funniest summer vacation that any boy has ever had when a mysterious monster is sighted in nearby Lake Ontario. (Bantam)

NON-FICTION BOOKS

THE ABOMINABLE SNOWMAN by Barbara Antonopulos (gr 3–6)

The great unsolved mystery of the strange, legendary creature who lives in the faraway Himalaya Mountains. (Field/Raintree)

ALI by Rex Lardner (gr 6–h.s.)

The exciting details of Muhammad Ali's rise to the top of the boxing world. More than sixty pages of photographs are included. (Tempo)

ANNE FRANK: THE DIARY OF A YOUNG GIRL (gr 7–h.s.)

13-year-old Anne Frank kept her *Diary* while in hiding with her family from the Nazis. The book is a moving observation of the horrors going on about her as well as her own personal feelings about growing up. (Washington Square Press/Doubleday)

THE BASEBALL BOOK by Zander and Phyllis Hollander (gr 4–8)

Here are the stars, the teams, the rules, the records, and the great games in the history of America's favorite sport. (Random House)

BASKETBALL'S MAGNIFICENT BIRD: THE LARRY BIRD STORY by Frederick Lynn Corn (gr 5–9)

The heartwarming story of the Boston Celtics' star whose skill and team spirit are outstanding. (Random House)

THE BERENSTAIN BEARS' SCIENCE FAIR by Stan and Jan Berenstain (K–3)

The Berenstain Bears teach young readers about the world they live in with projects and experiments and things to make and do. (Random House)

CHARLIE BROWN'S SECOND SUPER BOOK OF QUESTIONS AND ANSWERS by Charles Schultz (gr 3–5)

Where do stars go in the daytime? That question and many

more about the earth, space, and planets are answered here. (Random House)

CHEAPER BY THE DOZEN by Frank B. Gilbreth, Jr. and Ernestine Gilbreth Carey (gr 7–h.s.)

This hilarious story tells what happens when a family of twelve children is brought up by parents who are efficiency experts. (Bantam/Crowell)

CHEERLEADING AND BATON TWIRLING by Roberta Davis (gr 3–7)

This book tells how to be a great cheerleader and baton twirler: tips on appearance, preparation for tryouts, latest cheers, and more. (Tempo)

CHRISTOPHER COLUMBUS by Ann McGovern (gr 3–5)

Columbus' many explorations, including the discovery of America, are told in this book. (Scholastic)

THE COMPLETE BABY-SITTER'S HANDBOOK by Carol Barken and Elizabeth James (gr 4–9)

Here's everything a baby-sitter needs to know about how to get jobs and care for children with safety and confidence. (Wanderer)

CREATURES FROM UFO'S by Daniel Cohen (gr 4-8)

Here are strange, exciting tales of close encounters humans have had with creatures from outer space. (Archway)

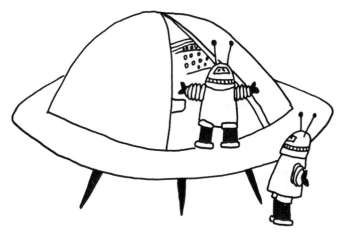

CROWELL BIOGRAPHY SERIES (gr 1—4)

This series tells the exciting life stories of famous Americans including Leonard Bernstein, Wilt Chamberlain, Jackie Robinson, Eleanor Roosevelt, and Jim Thorpe. (Crowell)

ENCYCLOPEDIA BROWN'S RECORD BOOK OF WEIRD AND WONDERFUL FACTS by Donald J. Sobol (gr 3—7)

Encyclopedia Brown, the popular young detective, takes readers on a fascinating tour of true and amazing facts. (Dell/Delacorte)

JEAN FRITZ BOOKS (gr 2—6)

Here are six humorous and historically accurate biographies about famous personalities from the colonial past. The author's sparkling writing style makes history fresh, interesting, and alive in this series. Titles include *And Then What Happened, Paul Revere?, Can't You Make Them Behave, King George?, What's The Big Idea, Ben Franklin?, Where Was Patrick Henry on the 29th of May? Why Don't You Get a Horse, Sam Adams?,* and *Will You Sign Here, John Hancock?* (Putnam Publishing Group)

GREAT PETS! by Sara Stein (gr 3—8)

An exciting guide packed with information about more than fifty common and unusual household pets. (Workman)

GARFIELD: THE COMPLETE CAT BOOK by Shep Steneman (gr 5–8)

Garfield, the cartoon cat, narrates this book about cat breeds, cat care, and much more for cat lovers to read and enjoy. (Random House)

GIRL TALK by Molly Douglas (gr 6–9)

A complete guide to beauty, fashion, and health for girls. (Field/Acropolis)

THE GUINNESS BOOK OF WORLD RECORDS by Norris and Ross McWhirter (gr 7–h.s.)

The world's greatest record-breakers are listed in this collection. (Bantam)

HARRIET TUBMAN: CONDUCTOR ON THE UNDERGROUND RAILWAY by Ann Petry (gr 7–h.s.)

Harriet Tubman, born a slave on a Maryland plantation, grew up to inspire and lead over 300 men, women, and children through the dangerous escape route to the North known as the underground railroad. (Archway/Crowell)

HARRY HOUDINI MASTER OF MAGIC by Robert Kraske (gr 4–6)

The incredible story of Houdini, the world's greatest escape artist. (Scholastic)

HOW DID IT BEGIN? by Lewis K. Parker (gr 4–6)

Imagine life without M & M's, jeans, and potato chips. They weren't always here. This book is full of great stories of how our favorite things came to be. (Field)

HOW KIDS CAN REALLY MAKE MONEY by Shari Lewis (gr 3–6)

This useful book suggests new and practical ways to earn money including raising and caring for animals, starting a baby-sitting business, and running a rent-a-kid service for older folks. (Holt, Rinehart & Winston)

IF YOU LIVED IN COLONIAL TIMES by Ann McGovern (gr 3–5)

Many questions, answers, and pictures about what life was like in the American colonies. (Scholastic)

KID'S AMERICA by Steven Caney (gr 3–7)

A huge catalog jam-packed with activities, projects, and delightful information for children. (Workman)

LIONEL RICHIE by Roberta Plutzik (gr 7–h.s.)

Here is the illustrated inside story of Lionel Richie, one of pop music's charismatic superstars. (Dell)

THE LUCK BOOK by Maria Leach (gr 4-7)

This humorous book describes the many surprising things that people do all over the world for good luck — from wishing on a star to carrying a lucky penny in a shoe. (Dell)

MARTIN LUTHER KING: THE PEACEFUL WARRIOR by Ed Clayton (gr 4–6)

The courageous and inspiring biography of the hero of the civil rights movement. (Archway/Prentice-Hall)

MAGIC SCIENCE TRICKS by Dinah Moche (gr 3-6)

Young magicians can learn how to do mystifying tricks with

ordinary items found at home. (Scholastic)

MARY LOU RETTON by George Sullivan (gr 6–h.s.)

Here is the exciting story of Mary Lou Retton, first American woman to win an Olympic Gold medal in gymnastics. (Wanderer)

MAX: THE DOG THAT REFUSED TO DIE by Kyra P. Wayne (gr 4–6)

Max, a Doberman, is chasing a squirrel in the Sierras when he suddenly falls from a cliff and is badly injured. Incredibly, Max lives to find his beloved owners. (Field/Alpine)

MR. WIZARD'S SUPERMARKET SCIENCE by Don Herbert (gr 4–7)

TV's Mr. Wizard shows more than 100 fun-to-do science experiments and tricks that use everyday items found in the supermarket. (Random House)

THE MONSTER OF LOCH NESS by James Cornell (gr 6–9)

Is the Loch Ness Monster a hoax or a strange beast? Photos, drawings, and details of scientists' findings. (Scholastic)

MONSTERS FROM THE MOVIES by Thomas G. Aylesworth (gr 5-8)

How many monster movie fans know that Thomas Edison made America's first Frankenstein film or that King Kong has a son? This book is crammed with fascinating facts and sensational secrets about the world's most terrifying movie monsters. (Bantam)

MY VISIT TO THE DINOSAURS by Aliki (K–3)

Young readers are invited on a trip to a museum's hall of dinosaurs where they can visit the giant creatures who ruled the earth millions of years ago. (Harper)

ON THE TRACK OF BIGFOOT by Marian T. Place (gr 5–h.s.)

The intriguing story of the search for the strange man-like creatures in the dense forests of the Pacific Northwest. (Archway/Dodd, Mead)

POCAHONTAS, INDIAN PRINCESS by Katherine Wilkie (gr 2–5)

The true story of the brave Indian princess who helped the settlers of the first English colony in the New World to survive their first winter here. (Field/Garrard)

ROMANCE! CAN YOU SURVIVE IT? by Meg Schneider (gr 7–h.s.)

This helpful guide teaches how to handle difficult dating situations. (Dell)

SCHOLASTIC FUNFACT BOOKS (gr 4–6)

These books offer information about intriguing subjects. Included in this series are books about dinosaurs, ghosts, monsters, prehistoric beasts, space flights, UFO's, and underwater worlds. (Scholastic)

THE SCIENCE BOOK by Sara Stein (gr 4–7)

The Science Book is filled with terrific discoveries, dazzling experiments, and clear explanations about unusual natural phenomena. (Workman)

SHE WANTED TO READ by Ella Kaiser Carruth (gr 3-7)

Mary McLeod Bethune grew up on a cotton plantation in South Carolina and was the first in her family who could read or write. Here is the inspiring story of how this young girl dedicated her life to help black children gain an education. (Archway/Abingdon)

SKATEBOARDS AND SKATEBOARDING: THE COMPLETE BEGINNER'S GUIDE by La Vida Weir (gr 7–9)

This fun-filled illustrated book teaches how to make and safely ride skateboards. (Bantam)

THE STORY OF THOMAS ALVA EDISON by Margaret Davidson (gr 3–5)

The biography of America's amazing inventor, best-remembered for the electric light, moving pictures, and the phonograph. (Random House)

THE SUPERMAN BOOK OF SUPERHUMAN ACHIEVEMENTS by Shep Steneman (gr 3–7)

America's favorite superhero presents more than 100 of history's most astonishing record-breaking events. (Random House)

THE TALLEST LADY IN THE WORLD by Norah Smaridge (gr 3–6)

The amazing story of how The Statue of Liberty came to stand in New York Harbor over 100 years ago. (Field)

THINGS KIDS COLLECT! by Shari Lewis (gr 3–6)

Kids can have fun and become successful treasure hunters by collecting more than 25 different collectibles such as rocks, comics, dolls, miniatures, records, stamps, and stickers. (Holt, Rinehart & Winston)

TO ELVIS WITH LOVE by Lena Canada (gr 7-9)

Superstar Elvis Presley helps make a lonely, crippled girl's dream come true. (Scholastic/Everest)

TOM SEAVER'S BASEBALL CARD BOOK by Tom Seaver with Alice Siegel (gr 5–8)

Tom Seaver, the famous baseball pitcher, gives tips and advice on how to have fun collecting baseball cards. (Wanderer)

UFO ENCOUNTERS by Rita Golden Gelman and Marcia Seligson (gr 4–6)

Many of the most famous UFO sightings are described here. (Scholastic)

THE VALUE TALES (gr 1–5)

The *Value Tales* are exceptional books which present the fascinating stories of outstanding men and women from history. Each book in the series provides an understanding of the background and hardships these famous individuals faced, as well as the value or quality they have inspired in others. The collection includes *The Value of Believing in Yourself – Louis Pasteur, Adventure – Sacagawea, Caring – Eleanor Roosevelt, Courage– Jackie Robinson, Creativity – Thomas Edison, Curiosity – Christopher Columbus, Dedication – Albert Schweitzer, Determination – Helen Keller, Helping – Harriet Tubman, Honesty – Confucius,* and 18 other titles. (Oak Tree/Grolier)

VANISHED! by Wayne R. Coffey (gr 4–6)

Here are true stories of people who disappeared mysteriously. (Field)

WINNERS UNDER 21 by Phyllis and Zander Hollander (gr 4–8)

The twelve champions here won top honors in their sports before the age of twenty-one. This book reports the struggles and triumphs of Muhammad Ali, Tracy Austin, John McEnroe, Steve Cauthen, and other young sports stars. (Random House)

THE WORLD'S MOST FAMOUS GHOSTS by Daniel Cohen (gr 4-7)

Do ghosts haunt the living? Is the White House really haunted by the ghost of Abraham Lincoln? This book investigates many famous ghost stories from around the world and comes up with a good deal of interesting evidence. (Archway/Dodd, Mead)

WRESTLING SUPERSTARS by Daniel and Susan Cohen (gr 6–h.s.)

Wrestling fans can find everything they want to know about the lives and careers of dozens of the biggest stars in wrestling. More than 35 pages of photographs are included. (Archway)

YOUR OWN SUPER MAGIC SHOW by Marvin Miller (gr 2–4)

This book contains eight great punch-out magic tricks, plus the props needed to perform them. (Scholastic)

PUBLISHERS' DIRECTORY

ABINGDON BOOKS, 201 Eighth Avenue South, Nashville, Tennessee 37202

ACROPOLIS BOOKS, 2400 17th Street, N.W., Washington, D.C. 20009

ALPINE PUBLISHERS, 1901 South Garfield Street, Loveland, Colorado 80537

ARCHWAY PAPERBACKS, Pocket Books, 1230 Avenue of the Americas, New York, N.Y. 10020

ATHENEUM PUBLISHERS, 115 Fifth Avenue, New York, N.Y. 10003

AVON BOOKS, 1790 Broadway, New York, N.Y. 10019

BANTAM BOOKS, 666 Fifth Avenue, New York, N.Y. 10019

BERKLEY BOOKS, 200 Madison Avenue, New York, N.Y. 10010

BRADBURY PRESS, MacMillan Publishing Company, 866 Third Avenue, New York, N.Y. 10022

CONTEMPORARY PERSPECTIVES, 230 East 48th Street, New York, N.Y. 10017

CROWELL BOOKS, Harper & Row, 10 East 53rd Street, New York, N.Y. 10022

DEL REY BOOKS, Ballantine Books, 201 East 50th Street, New York, N.Y. 10022

DIAL PRESS, E.P. DUTTON PUBLISHERS, 2 Park Avenue, New York, N.Y. 10016

DODD, MEAD & COMPANY, 79 Madison Avenue, New York, N.Y. 10016

DOUBLEDAY, 501 Franklin Avenue, Garden City, N.Y. 11530

E.P. DUTTON PUBLISHERS, 2 Park Avenue, New York, N.Y. 10016

FARRAR, STRAUS, & GIROUX, 19 Union Square West, New York, N.Y. 10003

FIELD PUBLICATIONS, 245 Long Hill Road, Middletown, Connecticut 06457 (Please note that the titles from this publisher are available only through Weekly Reader School Books Clubs)

GARRARD PUBLISHING COMPANY, 29 Goldsborough Street, Easton, Maryland 21601

GOLDEN PRESS, Western Publishing Company, 850 Third Avenue, New York, N.Y. 10022

GROLIER ENTERPRISES, Sherman Turnpike, Danbury, Connecticut 06816

GROSSET & DUNLAP, Putnam Publishing Group, 200 Madison Avenue, New York, N.Y. 10016

HARCOURT BRACE JOVANOVICH, 111 Fifth Avenue, New York, N.Y. 10003

HARPER BOOKS, Harper & Row, 10 East 53rd Street, New York, N.Y. 10022

HOLT, RINEHART, AND WINSTON, 383 Madison Avenue, New York, N.Y. 10017

HOUGHTON MIFFLIN, 2 Park Street, Boston, Massachusetts 01803

ALFRED A. KNOPF, RANDOM HOUSE, INC., 201 East 50th Street, New York, NY 10022

LODESTAR BOOKS, 2 Park Avenue, New York, N.Y. 10016

MEADOWBROOK PRESS, 18318 Minnetonka Boulevard, Deephaven, Minnesota 55391

WILLIAM MORROW & COMPANY, 2 Park Avenue, New York, N.Y. 10016

OAK TREE PUBLICATIONS, 9601 Aero Drive, San Diego, California 92123

PENDULUM PRESS, Academic Building, Saw Mill Road, West Haven, Connecticut

PHILOMEL, 200 Madison Avenue, Suite 1045, New York, N.Y. 10015

POCKET BOOKS, 1230 Avenue of the Americas, New York, N.Y. 10020

PRENTICE-HALL, INC., Englewood Cliffs, New Jersey 07632

PUFFIN BOOKS, Penguin Books, 40 West 23rd Street, New York, N.Y. 10010

PUTNAM PUBLISHING GROUP, 200 Madison Avenue, New York, N.Y. 10016

RAINTREE PUBLISHERS, 330 East Kilbourn Avenue, Milwaukee, Wisconsin 53202

RANDOM HOUSE, INC., 201 East 50th Street, New York, N.Y. 10022

SCHOLASTIC BOOK SERVICES, 730 Broadway, New York, N.Y. 10003

SIGNET BOOKS, 1633 Broadway, New York, N.Y. 10019

SIMON & SCHUSTER, 1230 Avenue of the Americas, New York, N.Y. 10020

TEMPO BOOKS, Putnam Publishing Group, 200 Madison Avenue, New York, N.Y. 10016

VIKING PRESS, 40 West 23rd Street, New York, N.Y. 10010

WALLABY BOOKS, Pocket Books, 1230 Avenue of the Americas, New York, N.Y. 10020

WANDERER BOOKS, Simon & Schuster, 1230 Avenue of the Americas, New York, N.Y. 10020

WASHINGTON SQUARE PRESS, 1230 Avenue of the Americas, New York 10020

WORKMAN PUBLISHING COMPANY, 1 West 39th Street, New York, N.Y. 10018

WORKBOOKS

Some of the workbooks listed here have been designed to be used by children in school. All of these workbooks can be an effective part of your vocabulary-building program at home. You can write to the publishers to order single copies of those books which interest you.

AMSCO SCHOOL PUBLICATIONS, 315 Hudson Street, New York, N.Y. 10013

Adventures with Words (gr 7–h.s.)
101 Ways to Learn Vocabulary (gr 8–h.s.)
Reading, Spelling, Vocabulary, Pronunciation (gr 4–7)
Vocabulary Through Pleasurable Reading (gr 6–8)
Words at Work (gr 8–h.s.)

BARRON'S EDUCATIONAL SERIES, 113 Crossways Park Drive, Woodbury, N.Y. 11797

504 Absolutely Essential Words (gr 7–h.s.)
1100 Words You Need to Know (gr 7–h.s.)
Vocabulary Builder (gr 7–h.s.)

GLOBE BOOK COMPANY, 50 West 23rd Street, New York, N.Y. 10010

World of Vocabulary Series (gr 5–h.s.)

HAMMOND, INC., 515 Valley Street, Maplewood, N.J. 07040

Words Are Important (gr 4–h.s.)

MODERN CURRICULUM PRESS, 13900 Prospect Road, Cleveland, Ohio 44136

Building Language Power with Cloze (gr 2–6)
Building Word Power (gr 2–6)
High Action Reading for Vocabulary (gr 2–6)

RANDOM HOUSE PUBLISHERS, 400 Hahn Road, Westminster, Maryland 21157

Practicing Vocabulary in Context (gr 2–8)
Skill Builders Series (gr 1–6)
Spotlight on Vocabulary (gr 3–8)

SADLIER-OXFORD, 11 Park Place, New York, N.Y. 10007

Using Words with Competency (gr 4–7)
Vocabulary Workshop (gr 6–9)

SCHOOLHOUSE PRESS, 4700 Rockside Road, Independence, Ohio 44131

Vocabulary Works (gr 2–6)
The Word Book (gr 1–2)

SCHOLASTIC BOOKS, 730 Broadway, New York, N.Y. 10003

Practical Vocabulary (gr 6–9)
Trackdown (gr. 6–9)
Vocabulary Improvement (gr 6–9)
Word Power (gr. 6–9)

WORD PUZZLE BOOKS

DOUBLEDAY & COMPANY, 501 Franklin Avenue, Garden City, N.Y. 11530

Beginner's Crossword Book (gr 4–7)
Crossword Carnival (gr 3–4)
Crosswords Around the U.S.A. (gr 3–4)
Crosswords for Kids (gr 7–9)
Introduction to Crossword Puzzles (gr 4–7)

FEARON-PITMAN, 6 Davis Drive, Belmont, California 94002

Word Puzzles (gr 3–5)

FIELD PUBLICATIONS, 245 Long Hill Road, Middletown, Connecticut 06457 (These puzzle books are available only through Weekly Reader School Book Clubs)

A-Team Activity Action Book (gr 1–3)
Braingames Activity Book (gr 2–3)
Dinosaur Fun Book (K–2)
Frosty the Snowman's Activity Book (gr 1–3)
Gummi Bears Activity Fun (K–2)
Hidden Words Fun-Find Puzzles (gr 3–6)
Scooby-Doo Happytime Fun Pad (K-3)

PUTNAM PUBLISHING GROUP, 200 Madison Avenue, New York, N.Y. 10016

The Flintstones Activity and Fun Book (gr 1–3)
Practice-At-Home Activity Book (K–2)
Santa Mouse Puzzle Pencil Fun (K–2)
Snake Tales Pencil Puzzle Book (gr 1–3)

RANDOM HOUSE, INC., 201 East 50th Street, New York, N.Y. 10022

Encyclopedia Brown's Book of Puzzles and Games (gr 3–7)
Sports Teasers: A Book of Games and Puzzles (gr 5–8)
The Three Investigators' Book of Mystery Puzzles (gr 3–7)

SCHOLASTIC BOOKS, 730 Broadway, New York, N.Y. 10003

Charlie Brown's All Sports Crossword Puzzles (gr 3–5)

Crackerjack Crosswords (gr 4–6)
Flintstones: Stone-Age Crosswords (gr 4–6)
Ghostbusters Puzzle Fun Book (gr 6–8)
Marmaduke's Puzzle Book (gr 6–8)
Mr. Magoo's Far-Sighted Fun (gr 4–6)
Peanuts Around the World Crossword Puzzles (gr 3–5)
Peanuts Holiday Crossword Puzzles (gr 3–5)
Puzzle Time (gr 4–6)

Children of all ages like to do word-search
games and crossword puzzles.

9

Magazines For Young People

You will find many magazines listed in this section that will stretch your child's imagination and make reading fun. Before you actually subscribe to any magazine, make sure that it appeals to your child. You will also want to find out whether special introductory subscription rates are available for new subscribers.

Most magazines included here can be found in your local library or at your neighborhood newsstand. If you cannot find some of these magazines, you can request sample copies. Many publishers are delighted to send free copies of their magazines to potential subscribers.

Here is a letter that you might use to make your request:

your street address
city, state, zip code
date

Dear_____ Magazine:

Your magazine has been brought to my attention, and I am planning to enter a subscription for my *(son or daughter)*. However, I have not been able to find a copy of your magazine to show to my child. I would greatly appreciate your sending me a sample copy along with current subscription rates. Thank you.

Very truly yours,

(your name)

In the magazine descriptions which follow, you will find the grade level and interest appeal of each magazine written in parentheses after the title. For example, (gr 3–7) means that children in third through seventh grade would enjoy that particular magazine.

Subscription rates are continually changing. Do not rely on the yearly subscription rates given in the listings, for these rates may no longer be in effect.

Magazines stretch a child's imagination and make reading fun.

MAGAZINES FOR YOUNGER CHILDREN

BOYS' LIFE (gr 3–8)

Boys will find many articles here on outdoor life, nature, camping, science, and sports. On the lighter side, there are cartoons, hobby projects, and jokes.

Boy Scouts of America, 1325 Walnut Hill Lane, Irving, Texas 75038 ($13.20/12 issues)

CHILD LIFE (gr 2–8)

Child Life calls itself a mystery and science-fiction magazine. In addition to suspenseful mystery and adventure stories, readers can find articles about sports and crafts, recipes, puzzles, and jokes.

Child Life, 1100 Waterway Boulevard, P.O. Box 567, Indianapolis, Indiana 42602 ($11.95/8 issues)

CHILDREN'S DIGEST (gr 3–6)

This magazine offers excellent short stories and non-fiction articles. There are also puzzles, riddles, games, and crafts.

Children's Digest, 1100 Waterway Boulevard, P.O. Box 567, Indianapolis, Indiana 46206 ($11.95/8 issues)

CHILDREN'S PLAYMATE (gr 1–4)

Stories, arts and crafts activities, simple science experiments, and puzzles are included in this colorful magazine for younger children.

Children's Playmate Magazine, 1100 Waterway Boulevard, P.O. Box 567, Indianapolis, Indiana 46206 ($11.95/8 issues)

CRICKET MAGAZINE (gr 2–7)

There is much good reading here to satisfy a child's many interests: fantasy, science fiction, biographies, poems, animal stories, sports and travel articles.

Open Court Publishing Company, 315 Fifth Street, Peru, Illinois 61354 ($22.50/12 issues)

EBONY JR! (gr 1–7)

This magazine focuses on developing children's pride in black culture. There are many exciting stories here about celebrities and historical figures, and also games, short stories, recipes, and arts and crafts.

Ebony Jr.!, 1820 S. Michigan Avenue, Chicago, Illinois 60605 ($8.00/10 issues)

ELECTRIC COMPANY MAGAZINE (gr 1–4)

"Sesame Street" graduates will enjoy this creative magazine which contains puzzles, jokes, cut-outs, and entertaining stories.

Electric Company Magazine, P.O. Box 2924, Boulder, Colorado 80322 ($10.95/10 issues)

HIGHLIGHTS FOR CHILDREN (gr 1-5)

Highlights features appealing arts and crafts activities, short stories, and non-fiction articles.

Highlights for Children, 2300 West 5th Avenue, Box 269, Columbus, Ohio 43216 ($17.95/11 issues)

JACK AND JILL (gr 1–6)

Stories, articles, projects, riddles, and puzzles are included in this very popular magazine for young children.

Jack and Jill Magazine, 1100 Waterway Boulevard, Box 567, Indianapolis, Indiana 46206 ($11.95/8 issues)

NATIONAL GEOGRAPHIC WORLD (gr 3–7)

This magazine gives children an understanding of geography, travel, and faraway people and places.

National Geographic Society, 17th and M Streets, N.W., Washington, D.C. 20036 ($10.95/12 issues)

SESAME STREET MAGAZINE (preschool - gr1)

Big Bird and his friends bring the magic of the acclaimed TV series here in puzzles, cut-outs, and alphabet and counting practice.

Sesame Street Magazine, P.O. Box 2896, Boulder, Colorado 80322 ($10.95/10 issues)

YOUR BIG BACKYARD (preschool-gr 1)

This outstanding magazine includes colorful animal pictures, games, and interesting facts about the world of nature. A separate parent's guide is included with each issue.

National Wildlife Federation, 8925 Leesburg Pike, Vienna, Virginia 22184 ($10.00/12 issues)

PRE-TEEN AND TEEN MAGAZINES

ALFRED HITCHCOCK'S MYSTERY MAGAZINE (gr 7-h.s.)
This magazine features spooky mystery stories with surprise-twist endings.
Davis Publications, Box 1932, Marion, Ohio 43305 ($19.50/ 13 issues)

DANCE MAGAZINE (gr 8-h.s.)
Dance Magazine features news, people, profiles, and beautiful photographs from the sparkling world of dance.
Dance Magazine, Box 960, Farmingdale, New York 11737 ($23.95/12 issues)

DELL WORD SEARCH PUZZLES (gr 6–h.s.)
Dell proclaims that it is the "world leader in word searches." Each monthly issue contains hundreds of puzzles in which the reader has fun finding the hidden words.
Dell Publishing Company, Box 4800, Marion, Ohio 43305 ($12.50/12 issues)

EBONY (gr 6-h.s.)
Ebony is a picture magazine that covers every aspect of black life: current events, history, entertainment, sports, and fashion.
Ebony, 1820 South Michigan Avenue, Chicago, Illinois 60616 ($16./12 issues)

FANTASY AND SCIENCE FICTION (gr 7-h.s.)
Stories and novelets from outstanding science-fiction writers are presented here.
Fantasy and Science Fiction Magazine, Box 56, Cornwall, Connecticut 06753 ($16.97/12 issues)

HIT PARADER (gr 7-h.s.)
This magazine features articles about pop and rock music. Each issue also includes a "Parade of Hit Songs," with complete lyrics for dozens of popular songs.

Charlton Publications, The Charlton Building, Derby, Connecticut 06418 (22.00/12 issues)

JET (gr 6-h.s.)

Jet calls itself "a convenient-sized magazine summarizing the week's biggest black news." It covers important news in sports, music, personalities, fashion, and books.

Johnson Publishing Company, 1820 South Michigan Avenue, Chicago, Illinois 60616 ($36./52 issues)

MAD (gr 7–h.s.)

Mad is an outrageously funny humor magazine. It pokes fun at all aspects of our culture through its imaginative cartoons.

E.C. Publications, 485 Madison Avenue, New York, N.Y. 10022 ($10.75/8 issues)

READ MAGAZINE (gr 7-h.s.)

Read features appealing short stories and articles. Each is followed by practice exercises to build vocabulary and reading skills.

Xerox Education Publications, Box 16626, 4343 Equity Drive, Columbus, Ohio 43228 ($11.00/18 issues)

RIGHT ON! (gr 7–h.s.)

This magazine will appeal to fans of black stars in film, TV, records, and sports. There are many color photographs. Special features include record reviews and a pen pal address exchange.

Right On!, 105 Union Avenue, Cresskill, New Jersey 07626 ($13.95/12 issues)

SEVENTEEN (gr 7–h.s.)

This popular magazine for teenage girls features articles about fashion, beauty, and diet. It also deals with many of the real issues of teen life.

Seventeen Subscription Dept., Radnor, Pennsylvania 19088 ($13.95/12 issues)

16 MAGAZINE (gr 7–h.s.)

This teen fan magazine features articles about stars from the television and recording industries. The stories are gossipy and there are many photos.

16 Magazine, 157 West 57th Street, New York, N.Y. 10019 ($19.50/12 issues)

SONG HITS MAGAZINE (gr 7-h.s.)

The lyrics of approximately 60 or more pop, soul, or country hits are printed in each issue. There are also articles about well-known performers.

Charlton Publications, The Charlton Building, Derby, Connecticut 06418 ($17.00/12 issues)

TEEN MAGAZINE (gr 7–h.s.)

This magazine appeals to teenage girls. *Teen* features articles about hair styles, makeup, personal health and grooming. It also gives glimpses of television, movie, and recording celebrities.

Peterson Publishing Company, 8490 Sunset Boulevard, Los Angeles, California 90069 ($12.95/12 issues)

TIGER BEAT (gr 7–h.s.)

Tiger Beat calls itself the "biggest and largest selling teen magazine from Hollywood." The magazine contains many striking color photos, articles, gossip columns, and interviews with TV, film, and recording idols.

Tiger Beat, 105 Union Avenue, Cresskill, New Jersey 07626 ($13.95/12 issues)

YM

This girls' magazine, formerly called *Young Miss,* stresses greater self-awareness. It contains articles on good grooming, dating, career planning, fashions, and entertainment.

YM, P.O. Box 3060, Harlan, Iowa 51593 ($14.00/12 issues)

ANIMAL AND NATURE MAGAZINES

ANIMAL KINGDOM (gr 7–h.s.)

This magazine about animals reports on the habits and behavior of wild animals from all around the world. There are also many colorful photographs of various animals from microscopic creatures to elephants.

Animal Kingdom, Box 14267, Dayton, Ohio 45414 ($9.95/6 issues)

CAT FANCY (gr 5–h.s.)

This is a magazine for all cat lovers. Articles are presented about various breeds of cats along with their care and grooming. Two of the regular features are "Ask the Vet," and "Cats of the Stars."

Cat Fancy Magazine, Subscription Department, P.O. Box 2431, Boulder, Colorado 80322 ($17.97/12 issues)

OWL MAGAZINE (gr 3–7)

This magazine explores the world around us. There are pictures and posters of exotic animals, and stories of great discoveries and far-off places.

Owl Magazine, 255 Great Arrow Avenue, Buffalo, New York 14207 ($15.00/10 issues)

RANGER RICK'S NATURE MAGAZINE (gr 1–6)

The purpose here is to help children to enjoy nature and to recognize the need for conservation. Stories, articles, and craft projects are highlighted by many color photos.

National Wildlife Federation, 8925 Leesburg Pike, Vienna, Virginia 22184 ($14.00/12 issues)

SEA FRONTIERS (gr 7–h.s.)

This magazine is colorful and interesting in its presentation of all aspects of marine life and sea exploration.

International Oceanographic Foundation, 10 Rickenbacker Causeway, Virginia Key, Miami, Florida 33149 ($15.00/6 issues)

ZOONOOZ (gr 3–9)

This delightfully-written magazine tells about the animals and activities at the San Diego Zoo and Wild Animal Park. There are also many excellent photographs.

Zoological Society of San Diego, Box 551, San Diego, California 42112 ($10.00/12 issues)

HOBBY AND SPECIAL INTEREST MAGAZINES

COBBLESTONE MAGAZINE (gr 3–8)

This history magazine explores American's exciting heritage. Readers meet the men and women who helped to shape our country, and learn what it was like living in another time.

Cobblestone, 20 Grove Street, Peterborough, New Hampshire 03458 ($18.95/12 issues)

COINage (gr 7–h.s.)

This magazine for coin collectors features interesting articles about current and historic U.S. coins.

Miller Publications, 2660 East Main Street, Ventura, California 92002 ($14.00/12 issues)

COINS: THE MAGAZINE OF COIN COLLECTING (gr 7-h.s.)

This magazine presents the fascinating stories behind many U.S. coins and medals. It also reports on news from the Bureau of the Mint, and on the latest retail values of U.S. coins.

Coins Magazine, 700 East State Street, Iola, Wisconsin 54945 ($14.50/12 issues)

FAMILY COMPUTING (gr 6-h.s.)

Each issue includes reviews of software, shopping information about home computer systems, and programs for computers.

Family Computing, P.O. Box 2511, Boulder, Colorado 80302 ($15.97/12 issues)

FLYING (gr 7-h.s.)

This is the magazine for young people interested in learning how to fly and maintain small private airplanes.

Flying, P.O. Box 2772, Boulder, Colorado 80302 ($18.98/12 issues)

HOME MECHANIX (gr 6–h.s.)

This magazine focuses on do-it-yourself construction projects, and gives information about new inventions and gadgets.

Home Mechanix, P.O. Box 2827, Boulder, Colorado 80302 ($13.94/12 issues)

HOT ROD (gr 7–h.s.)

Hot Rod is the world's best-selling magazine about cars. Young people interested in cars, engines, and racing will enjoy reading about the basics of tune-ups and how to modify cars into hot rods.

Petersen Publishing Company, 8490 Sunset Boulevard, Los Angeles, California 90069 ($15.94/12 issues)

MODEL RAILROADER (gr 7–h.s.)

This magazine explores the miniature world of model railroading. There are many articles about railroad cars, locomotives, track lay-out plans, wiring, and mini-construction projects.

Kalmbach Publishing Company, 1027 N. Seventh Street, Milwaukee, Wisconsin 53233 ($22.50/12 issues)

MOTOR BOATING & SAILING (gr 7-h.s.)

This magazine is just right for boating and sailing fans. The articles range from boat design and care, to water safety and water sports.

Motor Boating & Sailing, Box 10075, Des Moines, Iowa 50350 ($15.97/12 issues)

MOTOR TREND (gr 8–h.s.)

There is plenty of up-to-date news here about current car models and those still on designers' drawing boards. Road test results are also given for domestic, foreign, and racing cars.

Peterson Publishing Company, 8490 Sunset Boulevard, Los Angeles, California 90069 ($15.94/12 issues)

ODYSSEY (gr 3–8)

Odyssey introduces children to the wonders of the universe, space exploration, and new developments in astronomy.

Odyssey, 1027 North 7th Street, Milwaukee, Wisconsin 53233 ($16.00/12 issues)

PENNY POWER (gr 3–7)

Penny Power uses cartoons, posters, and lively stories to give children important consumer information on the products they buy and use.

Penny Power, P.O. Box 2878, Boulder, Colorado 80322 ($11.95/6 issues)

POPULAR MECHANICS (gr 6–h.s.)

Young people interested in shop projects, cars, photography, electronics, and new inventions will enjoy this how-to-do-it magazine.

Popular Mechanics, P.O. Box 10064, Des Moines, Iowa 50350 ($11.97/12 issues)

STARLOG (gr 7–h.s.)

Starlog is filled with exciting information about science fiction movies, TV programs, and stars.

Starlog Press, 475 Park Avenue South, New York, N.Y. 10016 ($27.49/12 issues)

3-2-1 CONTACT (gr 3–8)

This magazine makes science fun and exciting with puzzles, projects, experiments, and questions and answers.

3-2-1 Contact, P.O. Box 2933, Boulder, Colorado 80321 ($11.95/10 issues)

SPORTS MAGAZINES

BICYCLING MAGAZINE

Bicycle enthusiasts can learn here about new products and equipment, repairs, touring, and advice for keeping fit.

Rodale Press, 33 East Minor Street, Emmaus, Pennsylvania 18049 ($15.97/10 issues)

CENTURY SPORTS DIGESTS (gr 6–h.s.)

This publisher monitors over 70 newspapers to locate the best stories and features written by top sportswriters across the U.S. In addition, interviews, sports quizzes, crossword puzzles, team rosters, schedules, and statistics are included. Publications include: *Baseball Digest* ($14.95/12 issues), *Basketball Digest* ($9.95/8 issues), *Football Digest* ($12.95/10 issues), *Hockey Digest* ($9.95/8 issues), and *Soccer Digest* ($7.95/6 issues)

Century Sports Digests, 1020 Church Street, Evanston, Illinois 60201

FIELD & STREAM (gr 6–h.s.)

Young sportsmen will enjoy this magazine's coverage of every aspect of fishing, hunting, and camping.

CBS Publications, 1515 Broadway. New York, N.Y. 10036 ($15.94/12 issues)

OUTDOOR LIFE (gr 6-h.s.)

The focus here is on outdoor recreation. Articles describe the adventure of fishing, hunting, and camping experiences.

Outdoor Life, Box 2851, Boulder, Colorado 80302 ($13.94/ 12 issues)

RUNNER'S WORLD (gr 7-h.s.)

This magazine brings up-to-date running news along with advice on how to train to be a fit and fast runner.

Rodale Press, 33 East Minor Street, Emmaus, Pennsylvania 18049 ($19.95/12 issues)

SKIING (gr 7-h.s.)

Young skiers will find articles here about skiing equipment, skills, fashions, and famous skiing personalities.

Skiing, P. O. Box 2777, Boulder, Colorado 80302 (9.98/7 issues)

SPORT (gr 6–h.s.)

Sport contains many human-interest articles about famous professional athletes.

Sports Media Corporation, 119 West 40th Street, New York, N.Y. 10018 ($12.00/12 issues)

THE SPORTING NEWS (gr 6–h.s.)

This weekly newspaper contains interesting articles about all sports. It is filled with stories, gossip about sports figures, statistics, and action photographs.

The Sporting News, 1212 N. Lindbergh Boulevard, St. Louis, Missouri 63166 ($39.95/52 issues)

SPORTS ILLUSTRATED (gr 7–h.s.)

The articles and columns here deal with the wide world of sports' personalities and activities. Many action photographs add to the exciting pace of this magazine.

Sports Illustrated, 541 N. Fairbanks Court, Chicago, Illinois 60611 (58.86/54 issues)

SURFER MAGAZINE (gr 7-h.s.)

This magazine presents how-to-do-it articles about surfing and information on where to go to find the best surf.

Surfer Magazine, P.O. Box 1028, Dana Point, California 92629 ($18./12 issues)

TENNIS (gr 8-h.s.)

This monthly magazine is recommended by the U.S. Professional Lawn Tennis Association. Readers will find articles about tennis personalities, tips on how to play well, and tournament results.

Tennis, P.O. Box 2039, Harlan, Iowa 51537 ($17.94/12 issues)

10

Free Reading
Materials For
Your Child

Many excellent reading materials are available free at your local
library. Encourage your child to explore the bookshelves for

Make good use of your local library.

exciting stories and non-fiction books to borrow. Don't hesitate to ask the librarian to make recommendations. Librarians are experts who know how to find the right books to match a person's interests. Libraries offer a wide range of useful materials. Show your child the location of the encyclopedias and periodicals such as magazines, newspapers, and pamphlets. These materials are very helpful in preparing reports for school. Your child's school library is another source of interesting books and periodicals. However, schools have other materials that you can borrow. The next time you visit your child's teachers, ask if you may borrow books from them. Most teachers have extra books and workbooks tucked away in their supply closets. Some are publishers' sample copies, while others are older books which are no longer used. A child can get valuable reading practice and learn many important words from these textbooks.

There are many interesting and informative free booklets available from corporations and government agencies. The best source of current free offers can be found in the paperback book entitled *Free Stuff For Kids*, which is published by Meadowbrook Press. Children really enjoy sending away for free things, and are thrilled to receive replies in the mail.

Your child might want to send for some of the free booklets and brochures from the following list. A request for any of these free items could be written on a postcard in this way:

> your street address
> city, state, zip code
> date

Dear *(name of company)*:

I would greatly appreciate your sending me a copy of your free booklet, *(name of booklet)*, at your earliest convenience. Thank you.

> Very truly yours,
>
> *(child's name)*

Several of these free offers require that a long self-addressed stamped envelope be enclosed along with your child's request. these listings say "be sure to enclose a long SASE."

THE ABC'S OF OIL

Oil and natural gas supply almost all of our energy needs and are also used to make every day products like nylon stockings, plastics, perfume, and even vitamins! This illustrated brochure shows how petroleum is found, brought up from the earth and refined.

Phillips Petroleum Company, Public Affairs Department, Bartlesville, Oklahoma 74004

BABYSITTING GUIDE

Everything you need to know to become an expert baby-sitter is right here! This terrific guide covers infant care, first aid, children's play patterns, the handling of temper tantrums, and much, much more.

Consumer Services, Johnson & Johnson Baby Products Company, Skillman, New Jersey 08558

BASKETBALL WAS BORN HERE

The world's first basketball game was played in Springfield, Massachusetts back in 1891. This 24-page booklet shows how a college professor's 13 rules for a new game became the popular sport of basketball.

Basketball Hall of Fame, Box 175, Highland Station, Springfield, Massachusetts 01109

BICYCLE SAFETY

More bicycles are being sold in the United States than automobiles! This valuable booklet gives basic rules for bike safety and tips for proper bike care.

Aetna Insurance, 151 Farmington Avenue, Hartford, Connecticut 06115

THE BIRTH OF A PENCIL

This illustrated 4-page brochure traces the history of the pencil back to the ancient Greeks and Romans. It also shows how pencils are made on today's factory assembly lines.

Berol U.S.A., Danbury, Connecticut 06810

BREAKFAST SCOREBOARD

Do you eat a good breakfast every day? This 4-page folder lets you keep score on how much energy your breakfast provides after a long night's sleep!

Kellogg Company, Department 0-2, Battle Creek, Michigan 49016

CATS

Cats are easy to care for, simple to housebreak, and fun to live with. This worthwhile brochure describes how cats can be perfect pets if they are treated properly.

Animal Rescue League of Boston, P.O. Box 265, Boston, Massachusetts 02217. (Be sure to enclose a long SASE)

THE CHILDREN'S ZOO

In this booklet younger children are taken on a lively tour of a children's zoo.

Public Relations Service, Eli Lilly and Company, 307 East McCarthy Street, Indianapolis, Indiana 46285

THE CONSUMER INFORMATION CATALOG

The current catalog from the U.S. Government contains more than 200 interesting publications (most are free!) Many brochures and booklets are listed about such subjects as automobiles, learning activities, food, health, recreation, travel, and hobbies. An easy-to-use order form is included with this publication.

Consumer Information Center, Pueblo, Colorado 81009

COOKING WITH SPICES AND HERBS

This 45-page handbook tells how to use over 75 spices and herbs to prepare exciting new taste sensations for your family.

Durkee Foods, 24600 Center Ridge Road, Westlake, Ohio 44145

COUNTERFEITING AND FORGERY

The counterfeiting of money is one of the oldest crimes in history. This informative brochure explains how to recognize counterfeit U.S. paper money and coins, and forged government checks.

Department of the Treasury, U.S. Secret Service, Office of the Director, Washington, D.C. 20223

DANCE EXERCISE

This easy-to-follow guide shows how dance exercise helps promote strength, flexibility, good posture, and better muscle tone. You don't have to be a dancer to benefit from dance exercise!

Capezio Ballet Makers, 1860 Broadway, New York, N.Y. 10023

DOGS

This 15-page pamphlet gives you some basic help for keeping your dog healthy and happy. (Be sure to enclose a long SASE)

Animal Rescue League of Boston, P.O. Box 265, Boston, Massachusetts 02117

DON'T MAKE WAVES

More than 47 million Americans currently enjoy some form of boating. Anyone who sails will appreciate this well-written and informative booklet about boating safety and etiquette.

Public Relations Department, State Farm Insurance Company, One State Farm Plaza, Bloomington, Illinois 61701

FINDING GOOD HOMES FOR PETS

What do you do if you find an abandoned or stray animal, or if your pet unexpectedly presents you with a litter of puppies or kittens? This brochure is filled with helpful suggestions on how to give those cats and dogs a better chance for long, happy lives.

Animal Protection Institute of America, P.O. Box 22505, Sacramento, California 95822

FOOD FROM THE SEA

This 48-page guide is chock full of facts on how to catch, prepare, and cook delicious seafood including clams, crabs, flounder, lobster, shrimp, and more.

Department of Marine Resources, State House Station #21, Augusta, Maine 04333

FUN EVENTS FOLDER

You and your friends can have a lot of fun raising money to help kids with muscular dystrophy. This fun-for-all kit explains how to plan a carnival, treasure hunt, bike race, bake sale, pet show, block olympics, magic show, and swim party.

Muscular Dystrophy Association, 810 Seventh Avenue, New York, N.Y. 10019

FUNDAMENTAL FACTS ABOUT UNITED STATES MONEY

American coins have changed many times since the country's first Mint was established in Philadelphia in 1792. This booklet describes the current types of U.S. coins and paper money, and how they are made.

Federal Reserve Bank of Atlanta, Atlanta, Georgia 30303

GROWING UP WITH CANADA

This booklet tells how the Canadian railroad network has met the challenges of helping to settle and develop Canada.

Canadian National Railways, Public Affairs Department, P.O. Box 8100, Montreal, Quebec, Canada H3C 3N4

GUIDE TO ANIMAL RIGHTS

There are 14 ideas outlined to help prevent the destruction of the animal kingdom. Literature describing the activities of the Animal Protection Institute is also included.

Animal Protection Institute of America, P.O. Box 22505, Sacramento, California 95822

HOCKEY RULE BOOK

Indoor hockey offers young people action, excitement, and competition. This booklet outlines the proper way to play, and includes special directions for the physically handicapped.

Cosom, 9909 South Shore Drive, P.O. Box 1426, Minneapolis, Minnesota 55440

HOW TO MAKE AND USE A PINHOLE CAMERA

This 12-page booklet from Kodak shows how to take real pictures by making your own camera from a tin can or old film cartridge. It's a great way to learn how a camera works!

Photo Information Department 841, Eastman Kodak Company, 343 State Street, Rochester, New York 14650

HOW PAPER COMES FROM TREES

Man has used paper to record his actions and ideas for centuries. This pamphlet describes how finished paper products are processed from trees.

Southern Forest Institute, 3395 Northeast Expressway, Atlanta, Georgia 30341

I LOVE HONEY

Do you know how hard bees work to make just one pound of

honey? About 556 honeybees must fly as far as 35,584 miles or more than once around the world! This interesting brochure explains how bees make honey and includes tempting recipes. California Honey Advisory Board, P.O. Box 32, Whittier, California 90608

INTRODUCTION TO SCALE MODEL RAILROADING

This 32-page booklet can help a model railroader create an accurate and appealing train layout in his home. Kalmbach Publishing Company, 1027 N. Seventh Street, Milwaukee, Wisconsin 53233

JOURNEY THROUGH A STOCK EXCHANGE

Here is a colorful cartoon story of how the American Stock Exchange works. Special sections teach young readers about stocks, bonds, and brokers.

American Stock Exchange, 86 Trinity Place, New York, N.Y. 10006

LURAY CAVERNS BOOKLET

Mother Nature has been at work for millions of years creating Luray Caverns in Virginia, a natural wonder deep within the earth. This booklet explains how Nature made the Caverns and includes fantastic color photos of amazing rock formations.

Luray Caverns Corporation, Attn: Public Relations, P.O. Box 748, Luray, Virginia 22835

MAN ON THE MOVE

This 64-page cartoon scrapbook surveys the history of transportation in the United States. Hundreds of fascinating facts illustrate how people have conquered distance with skill and imagination.

United Transportation Union, Public Relations Department, 14600 Detroit Avenue, Cleveland, Ohio 44107

THE MEN WHO MOVE THE NATION

Younger children will enjoy this 40-page educational cartoon coloring book about railroading.

United Transportation Union, Public Relations Department, 14600 Detroit Avenue, Cleveland, Ohio 44107

MICHAEL RECYCLE COMIC BOOK

This comic book will show you and your friends how to start a recycling program in your neighborhood. Here's how you can help the environment and also make a profit!

Reynolds Metals Company, Richmond, Virginia 23261

THE MIRACLE OF RUBBER

This booklet tells the amazing story of how Charles Goodyear changed the course of civilization by accident in his kitchen!

Public Relations Department, The Goodyear Tire and Rubber Company, Akron, Ohio 44316

It's exciting to get your own mail.

MR. PEANUT'S GUIDE TO TENNIS

Tennis anyone? Each day tennis becomes more and more popular. This useful booklet will help you understand the basic rules of the game and how to become a good player.

Standard Brands Educational Service, P.O. Box 2695, Grand Central Station, New York, N.Y. 10017

NEW YORK CITY VISITORS' GUIDE AND MAP

This brochure describes many exciting places of interest in the "greatest city in the world." Tourist attractions in each of the five boroughs of New York City are described here.

New York Convention and Visitors Bureau, 2 Columbus Circle, New York, N.Y. 10019

99 FACTS ABOUT THE FBI

How much do you know about the FBI? This valuable 32-page booklet tells how the FBI trains its agents, investigates serious crimes, captures criminals, and enforces the law.

U.S. Department of Justice, Federal Bureau of Investigation, Washington, D.C. 20535

THE OLYMPIC GAMES

Here is the fascinating story of the world's oldest and most spectacular sports competition. Sports fans can read about the history of the Games and how athletes are chosen for Olympic teams.

The U.S. Olympic Committee, 1750 East Boulder Street, Colorado Springs, Colorado 80909

PEANUT FUN AND FACT FOLDER

Peanuts are a fun food and pack a powerful punch too! Learn about the amazing history of the peanut, where peanuts are grown, and how to make your own peanut butter! (Be sure to enclose a long SASE)

Oklahoma Peanut Commission, Box D, Madill, Oklahoma 73446

THE POWER OF COAL

Did you ever wonder how coal was formed? This attractive booklet explains where coal is found, how it is mined, and how this resource will be used to provide energy in the future.

National Coal Association, 1130 Seventeenth Street, N.W., Washington, D.C. 20036

RICKY AND DEBBIE IN SARDINELAND

This color comic tells the story of how sardines are caught, processed, and canned. A mini-booklet of sardine recipes is also included.

Maine Sardine Council, P.O. Box 337, 470 North Main Street, Brewer, Maine 04412

RISING VOICES BOOK

The Carnation Company offers a special 210-page book filled with the important achievements of 52 outstanding Spanish-speaking Americans in government, sports, social service, and the arts.

Carnation, 5045 Wilshire Bouelvard, Los Angeles, California 90036

SAVING ENERGY COLORING BOOK

Younger children will have fun using this 16-page coloring book and learning about energy at the same time.

Whirlpool Corporation, Administrative Center, 2000 U.S. 33 North, Benton Harbor, Michigan 49022

SMALL PETS

Gerbils, guinea pigs, hamsters, white mice and rabbits are pets your whole family can enjoy. This booklet describes how to treat these small animals with loving care. (Be sure to enclose a long SASE)

Animal Rescue League of Boston, P.O. Box 265, Boston, Massachusetts 02217

SOLAR ENERGY FACTS

Are you curious about how to get power from the sun? You'll find descriptions and diagrams of ways to heat with solar energy in this booklet.

Research Products Corporation, 1015 East Washington Avenue, P.O. Box 1467, Madison, Wisconsin 53701

SPACE PRIMER

In the past 25 years, man has orbited in space, landed on and explored the moon, and sent spacecraft on incredibly long journeys to the sun and planets. This booklet clearly describes the development of man-made satellites, rockets, the Space Shuttle, and explains how people will live in space.

The Aerospace Corporation, P.O. Box 92957, Los Angeles, California 90009

SPROCKET MAN COMIC BOOK

Sprocket Man teaches bike riders safe-riding rules and survival skills in this 26-page comic book. Learn how to signal and make turns properly, avoid hazards, and stop safely.

U.S. Consumer Product Safety Commission, Washington, D.C. 20207

THE STORY OF CHECKS

Did you ever wonder how checks leave your hands and manage to come back to you? This cartoon booklet explains how checks pay for most of your spending.

Federal Reserve Bank of New York, New York, N.Y. 10045

THE STORY OF CHOCOLATE AND COCOA

You will learn the complete and fascinating story of where chocolate comes from, and how it is made into delightful delicacies.

Hershey's Foods Corporation, Consumer Relations, Att: Educational Mail, Chocolate Avenue, Hershey, Pennsylvania 17033

THE STORY OF THE TIRE

Did you ever wonder how rubber tires are made? This informative booklet describes the process in detail.

Public Relations Department, The Goodyear Tire and Rubber Company, Akron, Ohio 44316

TEXAS, LAND OF CONTRAST

This jumbo book (160 pages!) leads the reader through the fabulous state of Texas. Hundreds of color photos highlight the recreational, scenic and historical sights for the armchair visitor.

Texas Travel and Information Division, P.O. Box 5064, Austin, Texas 78763

THE THING THE PROFESSOR FORGOT

The Professor teaches younger children about the basic four food groups which are vital for good nutrition.

Consumer Information Center, Pueblo, Colorado 81009

TIPS FOR BETTER BOWLING

This booklet will show you now to improve your bowling scores. You will learn the right way to deliver the ball smoothly, to make spares, and to keep score.

AMF Bowling Division, Jericho Turnpike, Westbury, New York
11590

TIPS ON TOE SHOES

Young ballet dancers can learn how to select, wear, and care
for toe shoes from this illustrated booklet from Capezio.

Capezio Ballet Makers, 1860 Broadway, New York, N.Y. 10023

WATER SKIING FUNDAMENTALS

A beginning water skier can look like a champion by following the basic do's and don'ts outlined here. This booklet shows
the beginner how to practice on dry land before taking off in
the water.

American Water Ski Association, P.O. Box 191, Winter Haven,
Florida 33880

WOMEN IN AMERICA

The S & H Company offers a special 28-page booklet filled
with the important achievements of 70 famous women in
American history. These prominent women include writers,

scientists, civil rights leaders, reporters, politicians, artists, and musicians.

The Sperry & Hutchinson Company, Consumer Services, 2900 West Seminary Drive, Fort Worth, Texas 76133

YOGURT AND YOU

Everything you always wanted to know about yogurt is here in this illustrated 16-page booklet from Dannon – how it is made, why it is "naturally" good for you, how to shop for yogurt, and much more. Also included are exciting new yogurt recipes and fun ways to serve yogurt.

Dannon Milk Products, Department L2A, P.O. Box 1975, Long Island City, N.Y. 11101

11

Questions
And Answers

Here are answers to questions you may have about how to help your child get the most out of reading. You might want to read this chapter again before you begin your reading program at home

How can I help my child to become a better reader?

To encourage a child to read more – or to develop his reading skills to the highest level – reading must be enjoyable. Use this guide to help your child select books and magazines that sparkle with fun and excitement. The right reading materials will entertain your child for hours on end at home.

Why is WORD POWER the key to success in school?

Success in school depends to a great extent upon how well a child reads. Children with powerful vocabularies also have the best reading skills. These youngsters easily understand the information presented in their classroom work, homework assignments, and on reading tests.

Why is so much importance given to reading test scores?

Reading tests measure how well a child reads compared to other youngsters in the same grade. Many schools use reading scores as the basis for determining class placement. Schools generally group students into classes according to reading ability. In this way, an entire class can be taught at the same pace.

What is the purpose of giving my child a STARTER KIT?

This assortment of books opens the door to reading adventure at home. These delightful materials also provide an abundant supply of new vocabulary words for your child to discover and learn.

What should be included in a STARTER KIT?

Each KIT should include a novel, a non-fiction book about real people or events, a vocabulary workbook, a dictionary, and a spiral notebook. Recommended STARTER KITS for children in grades 3 through 9 are listed in Chapter 4 of this book.

Can I put together my own STARTER KIT?

The STARTER KITS described in this book contain popular paperbacks for each age group. However, feel free to substitute any book in a recommended KIT for another book with greater appeal for your child. (See Chapter 8 for alternate choices.)

Can I begin a reading improvement program by giving my child one book at a time?

You could begin in this way. However, giving your child the assortment of books in the STARTER KIT makes the beginning of your program an exciting, special occasion.

How will my child learn the meanings of new words?

Your child should circle each new word that he comes across in his reading and wants to learn more about. When he finishes reading, he should copy all the circled words into the notebook, and ask you or use the dictionary to obtain meanings for these new words. You and your child may want to discuss what each word means as it is used in the story.

Before your child uses workbooks or word puzzle books, go over the directions together for each new activity. Show

126

where the answers go and how to check them with the correct ones provided in the book. You can check any answers yourself that these books do not supply.

How many new words should my child find in each book he reads?

Let your child decide how many new words he wants to learn each day. A reasonable goal might be to find five or ten words in each chapter.

What if my child wants to circle and look up every new word he comes across?

Discourage him from this practice. It will slow down his reading and eventually cause him to lose interest in the program.

If a word has more than one meaning, how will my child find the "right one" in the dictionary?

Your child should look over the various meanings given for the new word and find the one meaning which makes the most sense in the sentence he is reading.

How much time should my child spend on the program each day?

Your child might begin by spending as little as fifteen minutes a day using the materials in the STARTER KIT. Let him increase his reading time when he wants to.

When should my child work on the program?

Decide upon a time of day that is most convenient for both of you. Your child should be able to read without interruptions. Try to be available at that time to answer any questions your child might have.

Why is it a good idea for my child to keep a daily record of his work completed in the back of the spiral notebook?

This practice will help your child keep track of his work and also give him a sense of accomplishment.

Should my child make up sentences containing the new words?

Your child will increase his understanding of the new words by using them in sentences. However, he should do this optional activity only if he enjoys it.

How can I develop my child's reading comprehension?

You might casually discuss your child's feelings about whatever he reads. Sharing your child's perceptions of characters, events, and ideas can enhance his understanding and appreciation.

You can begin by inviting your child to read to you or tell you about his favorite part of the story. You might talk about what events led up to that particular episode, and what's going to happen next.

A good approach here is to encourage your child to relate what he reads to his own experiences. You could, for example, ask your child if he agrees or disagrees with the actions taken by a character in a story. You can also encourage your child to compare his own family or friends, and neighborhood with those he discovers in books.

(For more information about the skills involved in reading comprehension, some helpful books are listed in the Appendix under "Parents' Guides to Reading Improvement.")

What should I do when my child finishes using the books in the STARTER KIT?

Replace those books with other appealing ones that your child can read comfortably on his own. Chapter 8 lists many outstanding paperback books for young readers. Read over the book descriptions with your child and select the new books together.

When is a book "too difficult" for a child to read?

Ask your child to read a page from the book. If there are five or more words on the page that your child is unable to read, you know that the book is too difficult.

How can my child learn new words from sources other than books?

Everyday experiences offer many opportunities to develop your child's vocabulary. Discuss the meanings of new words which your child hears in conversation, or on TV and radio. Encourage your child to learn new words from newspapers, magazines, comic books, educational games, advertising, souvenirs, and free booklets.

How can I measure my child's reading progress?

You will know that your reading program is succeeding when you notice that your child's
- reading habits change
- work and study habits improve
- report card marks go up
- scores on reading tests increase

How can my attitude help to make this reading program a success?

Work with your child in a cooperative, friendly way, and be sensitive to his needs and moods. Encourage him with sincere praise for good work. Have other family members do the same.

Be excited and confident that you are going to help your child grow as a reader. Your child will share your confidence and pick up your enthusiasm. Remember that this learning adventure is important, worthwhile, and will help your child take a giant step ahead in school and beyond!

Appendix

This section has been included for parents who would like to become even more involved in their children's reading progress. Most of the books listed here are available in inexpensive paperback editions, while some of the recommended book lists compiled by organizations are free upon request.

PARENTS' GUIDES TO READING IMPROVEMENT

Books and the Teenage Reader, G. Robert Carlsen, Bantam Books, 1980.

Choosing Books for Children, Betsy Hearne, Consumers Union, 1981.

Families Learning Together, The Home and School Institute, Simon & Schuster, 1981.

Hooked on Books, Daniel N. Fader, Berkeley Medallion, 1977.

A Parent's Guide to Children's Reading, by Nancy Larrick, Bantam Books, 1975.

Raising Readers: A Guide to Sharing Literature With Young Children, by Linda Lamme, Walker, 1981.

The Read Aloud Handbook, Jim Trelease, Penguin, 1982.

Reading, How To, Herbert Kohl, Bantam Books, 1974.

Your Child Can Read and You Can Help, Dr. Jane Ervin, Doubleday, 1979.

MORE RECOMMENDED READING LISTS FOR CHILDREN

Adventures with Books, by Shelton L. Root, Jr. and a Committee of the National Council of Teachers of English, Citation Press, Scholastic Magazines, Inc., 50 West 44th Street, New York, N.Y. 10036. Also available through the National Council of Teachers of English, 1111 Kenyon Road, Urbana, Illinois 61808.

Bibliography of Books for Children, by the Association for Childhood Education International, 3615 Wisconsin Avenue, N.W., Washington, D.C. 20016.

The Black Experience in Children's Books by Barbara Rollock, Dial Press, 1974. Also available through the Office of Branch Libraries, New York Public Libraries, New York Public Library, 8 East 40th Street, New York, N.Y. 10016.

Children's Books by Virginia Haviland and others, published by the Library of Congress. Superintendent of Documents, United States Government Post Office, Washington, D.C. 20402.

Children's Books and Recordings, Office of Branch Libraries, New York Public Library, 8 East 40th Street, New York, N.Y. 10016.

Children's Books of the Years, Book Committee of the Child Study Association, 50 Madison Avenue, New York, N.Y. 10010.

High Interest — Easy Reading for Junior and Senior High School Students by the National Council of Teachers of English, Marian E. White, Editor. Available from Citation Press, Scholastic Magazines, Inc., 50 West 44th Street, New York, N.Y. 10036.

Let's Read Together: Books for Family Enjoyment American Library Association, 50 East Huron Street, Chicago, Illinois 60611.

Notable Children's Books, by the Book Evaluation Committee of the Children's Service's Division of the American Library Association, 50 East Huron Street, Chicago, Illinois 60611.

Paperback Books for Children, Citation Press, Scholastic Book Services, 904 Sylvan Avenue, Englewood Cliffs, New Jersey 07632.

Reading With Children Through Age 5, Child Study Committee at Bank Street College, 610 West 112th Street, New York, N.Y. 10025.

RIF'S Guide to Book Selection, Reading Is Fundamental, L'Enfant Plaza 2500, Smithsonian Institute, Washington, D.C. 20560.

Index

About The Author

Len Kusnetz lives on Long Island with his wife and two children. He has taught English and reading for fourteen years in the New York City Public School System. He holds a Master's Degree in Educational Psychology from Teachers College, Columbia University, and a Bachelor's Degree from Rutgers University in American Civilization. He is currently involved in developing a writing skills curriculum for the New York City Board of Education, and is faculty advisor to an award-winning student newspaper. He has also taught test-taking techniques at York College.

Mr. Kusnetz is the older brother of Shelley Kusnetz, illustrator of this book.

SUPER BOOKS FOR KIDS

It's easy to begin a home reading program. Visit your local bookstore or use this convenient order form to put together a starter kit for your child.

☐ CHARLIE AND THE CHOCOLATE FACTORY
   by Roald Dahl (Bantam Books) $2.75
☐ TALES OF A FOURTH GRADE NOTHING
   by Judy Blume (Dell) $2.95
☐ E.T. THE EXTRA-TERRESTRIAL
   by William Kotzwinkle (Berkley) $3.50

☐ ENCYCLOPEDIA BROWN'S SECOND RECORD BOOK OF
   WEIRD AND WONDERFUL RECORDS
   by Donald J. Sobel (Bantam Books) $2.50
☐ RIPLEY'S BELIEVE IT OR NOT!
   30TH SERIES (Pocket Books) $2.50
☐ ENCYCLOPEDIA OF AMAZING BUT TRUE FACTS
   by Doug Storer (Signet) $3.50

☐ BUILDING WORD POWER
   by Alvin Kravitz and Dan Dramer (Modern Curriculum Press)
   ☐ Book C   ☐ Book D   ☐ Book E   ☐ Book F ... (each) $3.95
☐ 504 ABSOLUTELY ESSENTIAL WORDS
   by Murray Bromberg, Julius Lieb, and Arthur Traiger
   (Barron's Educational Series) $5.95

☐ CHARLIE BROWN ALL-SPORTS CROSSWORD
   PUZZLES (Scholastic) $1.50
☐ SUPER PUZZLE CHALLENGE (Scholastic) $1.50

☐ THE WUZZLE BOOK by David Gantz
   (Wanderer Books) $2.95

☐ NEW SCHOLASTIC DICTIONARY OF AMERICAN
   ENGLISH (Scholastic) $7.95
☐ THE MERRIAM-WEBSTER DICTIONARY
   (Wallaby Books) $9.95
☐ SPIRAL NOTEBOOK (80 pages, wide-lined) $1.95

☐ YOUR CHILD CAN BE A SUPER READER
   by Len Kusnetz (Learning House). $5.95

(also available at special discounts to parent groups and schools. For information write Learning House Publishers, 38 South Street, Roslyn Heights, N.Y. 11576)

Please send me the books
I have selected. I am

enclosing $ _____
in check or money order.
(Please add $2.40
to cover postage and handling)

N.Y. residents please include sales tax

To order by mail:

Super Books
Box 98
Learning House
Old Westbury, New York 11568

NAME _____

ADDRESS _____

CITY _____ STATE _____ ZIP _____

Please allow 4 weeks for delivery.